The most beautiful towns in

MEXICO

The most beautiful towns in
MEXICO

Author
NOEMÍ MARTÍNEZ LARGO

Photographies
ARCHIVO AGUALARGA EDITORES

Agualarga

NORIEGA
EDITORES

Agualarga

© AGUALARGA EDITORES, S.L.
Avda. Democracia, 7
28031 Madrid (España)

Rights reserved:

2001, EDITORIAL LIMUSA, S.A. DE C.V.
GRUPO NORIEGA EDITORES
BALDERAS 95, MÉXICO, D.F.
C.P. 06040
☎ 521-21-05
    01(800) 7-06-91
◀)) 512-29-03
✆ cnoriega@mail.internet.com.mx

Design
I+P ESTUDIO

Production
ISABEL RUBIO

© *Text*
NOEMÍ MARTÍNEZ LARGO

© *Photographies*
ARCHIVO
AGUALARGA EDITORES

Text editor
CAROLINA PIÑERO NIEVES

Translation
LOUIS FERNÁNDEZ

Photomechanic
SIGLO DIGITAL

Printing
VÍA GRÁFICA

Binding
LARMOR

ISBN for Mexico
968-18-6157-4

Legal Deposit
M-43626-2000

Printed in Spain

Introduction

Details de stone mural painting where elements of importance for Mexico, such as maize, are represented.

In this book dedicated to the towns of Mexico, we continue the trip initiated throughout the Mexican geography in a preceding work, which had a great reception, giving us encouragement to continue the dreamy excursion through these unending lands in order to show their cultural, artistic, historic, folkloric and gastronomic treasures which are the keys to open this Pandora like box, releasing, not the winds but the essential guidelines to enter this enigmatic world.

Sometimes, it is thought that the reality of a country life is written in the great stories, events and famous places but the person who lives intensively a huge and magical culture such as the Mexican knows that the essential reality of a country can be found in small details, such as a sample of craftsmanship made with lots of love and patience, a fruit stand or in the clean, wise and peaceful smile that its people offer to those who take the trouble to try to know and understand its daily life.

Fragment of wall painted with a street lamp decorated with stars and suns.

Wooden balcony over stone support.

Entrance to shop where we find hats of different kinds.

The pages that follow are full of towns which have as their main attraction their natural beauty and that of their surrounding landscape such as Ixtapan del Oro, located in an oasis of peace and greenness, morning mist and steep orography which contains areas still unexplored. Among these towns there is also the one called Omitlán de Juárez, located in one of the most suggestive zones of the state of Hidalgo with adequate areas for outdoor sports, fishing and mountaineering. Beauty and history are also found on Xochimilco, where prehispanic systems and traditions have survived which can be enjoyed as you travel in a "trajinera" decorated with flowers.

There are also towns whose traditions are found in the intrinsic Mexican cultural roots such as Papantla, which has made famous an old prehispanic cult, which worships the sun and fertility gods, known today as "Danza de los Voladores". This spiritual and traditional rite is surprising to those who watch it because the men who practice it, perform it taking turns tied to a light rope, fastened to a high post which appears as if they were truly flying. At Delicias we can find places of natural beauty, farms of several products and the "Museo de Paleontología" unique in the country.

Dreamy beaches and crystal clear waters that are an invitation to swim in them are main attractions in municipalities such as Paraíso whose history is older than it seems. Same characteristics of coasts and cliffs joined with the historic fact that it was the first mission founded in Baja California are the introductory card for Loreto, where you can enjoy delicious dishes prepared with marine products. Delicate agricultural goods, famous embroidery craftsmen products and the pleasant smell of its well-known guavas are some of the charms of the town of Calvillo. A beverage known and associated with Mexico throughout the world is named after the first town that produced it, Tequila, a place where you can visit several industries, which produce and market it. A history very close to Mexico and with places as pleasant as its spas, are present in the everyday life of Cuautla, located in the State of Morelos.

Colonial jewels of Mexican art typified by astonishing convents are found in Tlacochahuaya, such as the Convent of San Jerónimo, or Pátzcuaro, with numerous colonial buildings and a prehispanic tradition originated by the fact that it was an important city of the Purépecha culture.

Multicolored flowers of various kinds can be seen by passers by.

Interior of restaurant with a chair in the foreground.

Also connected with this culture are Tzintzuntzán, that has archeological remains to prove it and is near the Pátzcuaro Lake; other archeological remains of importance are kept in Tepotztlán and Comalcalco. The presence of prehispanic cultures has left its mark in the names of the streets of Ayapango, still known by their Indian denomination; there are samples of colonial architecture and delicious dairy products. In Metztitlán you can find valuable samples of local architecture as represented by the Santos Reyes Monastery. Yuriria has one of the most beautiful Augustinian convents in Mexico and is surrounded by a leafy and peaceful landscape.

Other towns are known among other things by the presence of rich mines that attracted those looking for wealth in previous times. This golden era is reflected on the walls of the homes, an era when remarkable buildings were constructed and the streets filled with life. It is still possible to recall among its streets samples of this heritage, giving it a special charm. El Oro is one of these places; here, you can visit the Museo de la Minería de México and see installations and tools used in other periods to mine and process the plentiful minerals of these lands. Real de Arriba is other mining town, with a beautiful church and a remarkable mountainous landscape. Something magic and which appears to come from the depths of the earth, invades the town of Xilitla, where a XVI century convent stands as well as the building complex known as "El Castillo" a dream come true which merges with the tropical landscape.

An unknown traveler who crossed the world with his few and modest belongings, without renown or publicity came to Mexico one day, never to leave again, explaining to those who met him that this was his country, that its land reached deep into his soul and that his breath was the breath of its people. This traveler, who arrived without reservations, was fascinated by the Mexican magic and atmosphere, a fact known by the population and which is shown with pride on their faces. This fascination with Mexico is what makes everything I write seem poor when I think of those corners touched by a magic wand. The total belief in what is expressed here is the reason for this book, which shows, with the clarity of words, at times powerless, faced with ideas originating in deep feelings some of the most interesting and surprising Mexican towns.

The author

Two story construction with bycolored pilasters.

Arcade topped by column, in white and yellow colors.

Delicias

CHIHUAHUA

This town, which has a suggestive name is attractive for many reasons, among them its modernity, popular, relaxed and comfortable atmosphere typical of towns despite having a large population and also for its neighboring natural beauties, which extend to the whole state of Chihuahua. This state is the largest in the country and has superb views such as Barrancas del Cobre, Paquimé, hugh frightening deserts, lakes and cascades which are among the highest in Mexico. Besides, Delicias may have contributed to clarify the prehistoric period of the world, thanks to the discovery of animals and fossils who lived millions of years ago in an inner sea surrounded by the exuberant vegetation growing in this zone.

One of the most beautiful spots in this state is precisely one that can be found in the area where Delicias is located, thanks to the crossing of Rio Conchos, one of the most important rivers in the state which

The building in the picture has arches formed with the same kind of stones as those on the pavement.

One of the streets of Delicias, with publicity billboards invading everything.

17

On the following page, *façade painted in various colors with a ceramic sun over the entrance arch.*

flows through a deserted terrain, forming cascades and dams and its water gives life to a variety of animal and plants. This young community is located in a territory that was previously part of Meoqui, Saucillo and Rosales, and due to the importance acquired because of its crops and farming activity the state congress created on January 7, 1935, the municipality of Delicias. Today, it remains one of the most important agricultural towns in its state, and, regardless of its recent creation, its beginning are traced to the end of the XIX century, when there existed in that place a station of Ferrocarril Central Mexicano. This line was used to carry agricultural products from an estate called Delicias, where famous quality vineyards were planted, which were replaced in 1943, by cotton plantations.

In its shield appear the agricultural symbols that make Delicias famous today; in the upper part there is a planted field presided by a large sun and in the lower half there are three cotton buds, a cluster of grapes and in the center a Greek column that represents culture and wisdom. Surrounding these images there is an inscription that reads: "Work, Loyalty and Perseverance". The layout of the streets answers to a planning made in accordance with modern tastes, following a project designed by Carlos G. Black; it is worthy of mention that, regardless of what one may think, the streets and buildings retain some of the characteristic flavor of older towns, and that the visitor does not seem to notice the modernity. Despite this, there are also buildings erected prior to the date of the town's foundation, such as Hacienda la Polvorosa, now Hotel del Norte, built by German immigrants in 1888 who devoted their energies to the steel, brewery and food industries. In the hotel there are still many original items which were part of the furniture and decoration of this house at the end of the XIX and beginning of the XX century, and which give it a special look. It is

Picture of the market where you can buy products of daily use.

Top part formed by medallions with figures of painted iron.

Town church with whitewashed walls and the towers with the group of bells.

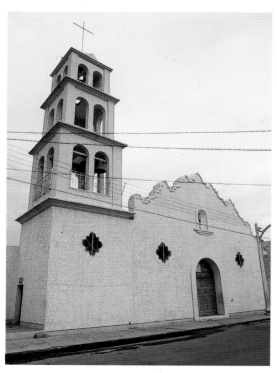

also interesting the former Estate of San Bartolomé, also known as Delicias, which was the cradle of the town and until 1930 one of its few constructions.

The important history and the circumstances of life in this place millions of years ago is evident in one of its best known attractions, Museo Paleontológico (Paleontological Museum), which is the most important one of its kind and which houses one of the most important fossil collections in Mexico. In what is today part of the State of Chihuahua more than 70 million years ago there was a large sea, and in it dwelled marine animals and plants, dinosaurs and other species of great interest to present day investigators. This mysterious period of life and history of the world, of which so much remains to be learnt, is now more familiar to us thanks to the high number of fossils and remains found in this area of Delicias. The collection is classified in marine and land invertebrates, minerals and meteorites and marine and land vertebrates, among which are included the dinosaurs and the mammoths. Apart from the remains found in the area and others in various parts of the country, there are some from outside Mexico. Mummies of Indians exhibited are also of great interest.

In the surrounding area, it is worth mentioning the Vado de Meoqui, on the banks of the San Pedro River, where it is possible to eat sea food and fish dishes, and Sauquillo, where it is possible to enjoy the marvelous natural sight created by quartz crystals known as Salón de las Espadas. The existence of thermal spring waters in an area formed by the rivers San Pedro and Conchos, has permitted the construction of two very pleasant spas known as El Delfín and the Junta de los Ríos. A trip through the gentle river Conchos in the boat named El Colibrí to the Rosetilla dam would be a good way to end your journey through the area of Delicias.

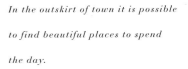

Shrine with the image of the Virgin surrounded by offerings and flowers.

Commemorative monument located in a leafy park with tall trees.

Details of a bridge built with stones.

In the outskirt of town it is possible to find beautiful places to spend the day.

Loreto

L oreto represents a page of the history of Mexico in a codex decorated with mountainous points, an impressive desert and a clear blue sea, which allows its insides to be seen because of its transparency. It is also light, sounds of birds that cut through the clouds to reach the sun, gastronomy and traditions. Loreto is all of these, a town located in the California peninsula and where the first mission was founded in 1697 with the name of Nuestra Señora de Loreto.

It is located across the Gulf of Mexico and includes places as Nopoló and Primer Agua, islands such as Monserrat, Danzante, El Carmen or Coronado and Puerto Loreto. This territory was previously known as Conchó or Conunchó and San Dionisio, but since 1697, after the arrival of the Spaniards, it was called Loreto in honor of the Virgin that they carried with them. The prehispanic dwellers were the Guaycuras,

The inscription on the door reminds you that Loreto was the first mission established in Baja California.

Buildings of Loreto, covered by vegetal fiber roofs.

23

Boats tied to the shore of the
promenade that enters the sea.

Detail of the façade with windows
that have the same shape as the
façade.

Façade of a wooden construction.

Façade of a store, decorated with
paintings and flowers.

Cabin facing the sea with an odd
decoration in front.

a people who left its mark in the traditions of this area. One of the
most surprising reminders of the cultures that lived in this place are
the cave paintings that are still kept in caves and rocks, of enigmatic
beauty and a meaning still unknown to us.

Loreto has always had a great historic importance due to the fact that
it is the first place where a permanent mission was established in the
California peninsula, although another existed in San Bruno since
1683. The foundation of Loreto was the most important and from it
began their missions Jesuits, Franciscans and Dominicans. The architectural complex projected included a church, a fortress and several
constructions used for different activities such as an army barracks.
At the start of the XVIII century a great storm provoked serious
damages to the buildings that had to be repaired slowly. In 1786 the
Jesuits who had settled there received an eviction order and were

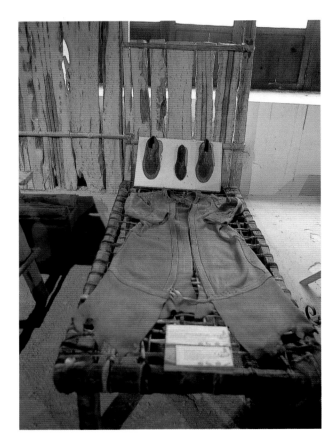

In Loreto you can see numerous objects related to the period of the missions.

replaced by Franciscans, who spent five years in Loreto, and by Dominicans.

History has also been nurtured in Loreto as it was for some time the capital of the two Californias, something that can be sensed in the landscape, the town corners and its people. To be in this town is similar to having crossed the tunnel of time and stopped in a past century, because of the constructions, which keep the original patina of its first period. Also, its people try to preserve its traditions and past, keeping the Museo de las Misiones in perfect condition, a museum which is located in the old homes of the priests and which houses important objects related to the activities and the world of missions. Apart from this place, are interesting the building where the municipal headquarters are located, the houses of the local people and the church of Nuestra Señora de Loreto.

The mission, surrounded by the buildings and homes of the municipality, was originally a fortified structure that housed a chapel where the

Promenade by the seashore, with steep mountains in the background.

On the following page, golden altarpiece and font with an interesting wooden cover.

Detail of some of the souvenirs that can be bought in the stores of Loreto.

image of the Virgen de Loreto was kept and several shacks. Later, the chapel was furnished with altarpieces and a tabernacle that arrived by boat. This area was growing and a house for different purposes was built near the church, all preceded by an atrium that later disappeared. The actions of nature such as storms, and earthquakes have provoked severe damages to the mission, losing some of its elements. Its portico is in renaissance style, very simple, having the upper portion and the bell tower been added later; inside it consists of a nave divided in five parts. The cover that can be seen today is product of a restoration which was carried out trying to give its original aspect; it is formed of wooden beams.

The artistic details of the church acquire a special beauty when they are illuminated by the dim light filtered through the windows; among them the best known is the image of Santa María de Loreto, situated in the main altar. Other important pieces are the fragments of an apostolate, images of San Bernardo or San Francisco, paintings such as *El Nacimiento de San Juan*, *La Coronación de la Virgen* and *Jesús*

Avenue leading to the beach, flanked by trees.

Loreto beach, with mountains and ships in the background.

Cabin built of painted wood with simple porch.

28

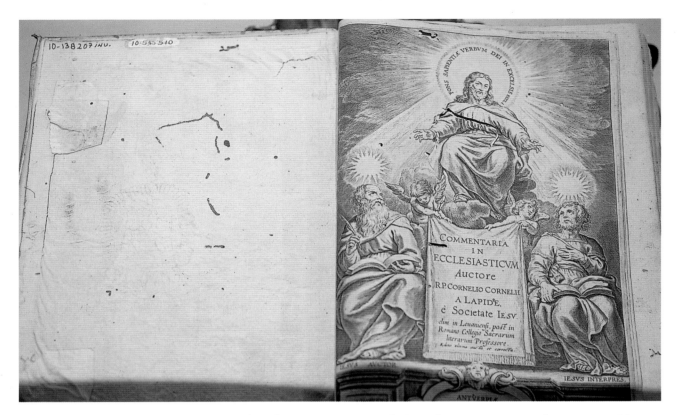

entre los doctores. As recorded in the inventories, the mission library had an important fund and there were important altarpieces, now disappeared.

Other attractions that can be enjoyed in this town and its surroundings are the mines where important quantities of minerals were extracted in the past, the Misión de San Javier, founded at the end of the XVII century, the caves with mural paintings and the many natural attractions such as the Oasis of Mulegé or the beach of Nopoló.

The presence of the sea is felt in the craftsmanship of the town, made with materials obtained from it. It is important to mention jewelry objects made with pearls and corals, shells and thread knits. The most typical dishes have fish and seafood as chief ingredients such as caldo de camarón (shrimp broth), almejada, langosta (lobster), almejas chocolatas del César, sopa de aleta de tiburón (shark fin soup), abulón or sopa de caguama (turtle soup).

Houses surrounded by palm trees
and other vegetation typical of its
climate.

On the following page, the limpid
blue color of the sky gives a sharp
contrast with the yellow of the walls.

Paraíso

In the region of Grijalva, State of Tabasco, is located a coastal municipalities limiting with the Gulf of Mexico in the North, so that it is a part of the coastal plain and lacks mountainous areas; it has 56 km of beach and large lagoons, among which are worthy of mentioning El Arrastradero, Eslabón, Tilapa or Mecoacán. Its climate is mild, almost as an eternal spring, favoring the existence of secondary jungle vegetations with exuberant plants and flowers. All these characteristics contribute to make this place a unique spot to enjoy nature, the sun, the beach and the sea, in surroundings that give the area the name Paraiso (Paradise) and that make it one of the most pleasant and visited seaside places in the State of Tabasco. The presence of a great variety of seabirds, such as tijeretas, gaviotas (seagulls), garzas (herons) or peregrinos, varied fish species from the sea and coastal

Residents of Paraiso in the street leading into the main façade of the church.

Arches in classic style with pilasters and highpoint arches, where taquerías and other businesses are located.

33

The combination of gay and
beautiful colors covers the façades
of Paraiso.

The streets of Paraiso have suffered
negative events but they have always
revived due to the strength of its
people.

lagoons, crustaceans and many species linked to the ecosystem of mangrove swamps.

This municipality, with a name that evokes dream worlds and objects, was established in a territory dedicated by the Jalpaneco people in 1823 to the timber industry, when they received permission from the Governor of the Department to do so. Halfway the XIX century it was a prosperous town, where cocoa and fruit trees were grown, being recognized mainly by its cocoa industry. The town began to grow, more houses were built, as well as a church with an open atrium and a square where tamarinds and laurels were planted. In the year 1872 Paraiso suffered a great fire that destroyed most of its buildings, but its inhabitants did not give up and began to rebuilt, stone by stone, the homes and other public buildings, according to a project prepared by Pablo Olivé and other professionals. This novel approach turned Paraiso into one of the best designs made in the state. In order to commemorate the reconstruction of the town, a monument donated by Manuel Sánchez was placed at the entrance of the square. The presence of oil in this area has contributed to attract more people as well as the cultural development.

The presence of waters with its beneficial consequences have contributed to the construction of spas which attract

Another street in town with a
bycicle-carriage and a small public
stand selling antojitos.

Pleasant image of a peddler and his
delicious fruit and vegetable
products.

Image of another corner of the town, as seen from the arcade.

In the background the garden full of vegetables typical of the zone due to its excellent climate.

many people searching for rest and peace during the year round; some of the best known are El Paraiso, Varadero and Pal Mar. All of them have adequate installations and rooms for visitors. Also this town attracts adventure lovers, as there are uncountable routes of interest because of the lagoons, its vegetation and fauna, apart from the river and the sea. Finally, apart from the important natural attractions of this town for its people and visitors there are various centers to practice or enjoy sports, especially Lienzo Charro, where you can see shows of charros, so famous and typical in this country. An installation which has a leading role during the Paraiso festivities, specially during the fair, is the Guillermo Sevilla Figueroa, which is equipped to hold the several expositions presented there.

Although it is a town open to changes and modernity, Paraiso does not forget its own traditions and has its popular culture always in mind. Among other things, this can be observed in its rich gastronomy, full of fish and seafood dished from Paraiso, apart from the typical dishes of the State of Tabasco. Also the popular expressions retain memories of past times and the musical activity is maintained alive through groups of drummers who play at popular, religious, social or private celebrations.

One of the greatest attractions of Paraiso is that of its white beaches with installations to make your visit a pleasant one.

Comalcalco

If we reach a municipality of the State of Tabasco surrounded by large plantations of cocoa and whose streets have a delicious smell of home made chocolate that waters the mouth, there is no doubt that we are in Comalcalco where there is also an important Mayan archeological zone and is the westernmost city of this culture and the first one where baked clay bricks were used for construction, due to the lack of stone. Its surprising and enigmatic buildings present some similarities with those of Palenque in the state of Chiapas and were built between the years 600 and 900 AD, belonging those to the Later Classic period; this magnificent city reached its maximum splendor in the Post Classic period, around the year 800.

This peculiarity of the construction material used in the prehispanic city gives the municipality its name, as Comalcalco comes from the náhuatl words *comalli* and *calli*, meaning "not too thick clay stone"

Commemorative statue of Licenciado Benito Juárez, next to a beautiful park surrounded by plants.

Colorful Comalcalco street, where street signs, advertisements, lights, and sounds mingle in an attractive combination.

In the foreground, one of many street stands offering a refreshment to the passers by.

On the following page, this photograph is evidence of the life and color flowing through the streets.

and "house" so that the name means "place of brick houses". The Mayans who inhabited this territory already had corn and cocoa farms that have remained until present times; with Comalcalco being one of the main producers of cocoa in its states; other products are avocados, rice, frijoles or zapote, the foundation of the town takes place on October 5th, 1827, when the state governor Marcelino Margalli issued a decree joining all the small ranches of the area under the name of San Isidro de Comalcalco. Soon afterwards, construction started of a church, the public square, the government building, a park, and lamp post were placed to give light during festivities and Sundays; also access bridges to the town were built, as the Santo Domingo or Doña María Cruz ones, the latter later known as Paso del Callejón de las Bailonas. After being raised to the rank of village, in 1897 a decree recognizes its importance, passing to the category of city and known then as Comalcalco.

This era can be traced in places and streets of the municipality in buildings as beautiful as the Cupilco church, but the sweetest places of Comalcalco are the cocoa estates where chocolate of known reputation is made one of the most important one is the Hacienda de la Luz, that was originally a still called Sitio Grande, and later called La Manchuria, before receiving the present name; in 1930, it was purchased by the German Otto Walter Hayer, who restored some parts and increased its facilities in order to convert it in one of the main cocoa estates of the region. The building known as Casa Grande and the gardens cover two hectares, there are 15 hectares of

Rose and violet colors are very common on the façades of Comalcalco.

Town gallery with portico.

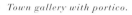

Among the numerous products of local craftsmanship you can find leather boots.

Peculiar monument combining iconographical Mexican traditions and time information.

pastures for cattle, 26 for cocoa cultivation and 5 where the original leafy vegetation is preserved. The building is constructed with bricks and different kinds of wood for the beams; the interiors present remarkable decorative designs made with mosaics and contain hand-made furniture, antiques tools, utensils and photographs. In the outside gardens there is a carefully selected variety of plants and fruit trees, both from the region and imported, some of which have great botanic value due to the risk of extinction. Since 1958, in this estate, chocolate has been manufactured from cocoa growing in its farms, protected by different types of trees. Today it is possible to visit the factory and learn its history, the manufacturing process and see its machinery.

The façade of the church is outstanding for its combination of colors and the height of its towers.

Details of the iron benches painted in white which decorate the street of Comalcalco.

When you watch in this period of history the impressive deserted buildings that shape the Mayan city of Comalcalco, it seems difficult to visualize the life that thrived once within its walls, the beauty of its better days and the meaning of inscriptions, hidden places, decorative details and images. To understand it, as it really was, can contribute the description given in 1881 by Desire Charnay, as many of its original elements have disappeared. Nine years after this, Pedro H. Romero undertakes the first excavations in the area, and in 1925 Oliver La Farge and Franz Blom, members of an expedition, made sketches, gave broader descriptions, and discovered the graves of the Nine Lords of the Night. Later investigations and excavations have

continued, allowing the confirmation of the historical and archaeological importance of the city. At its entrance there is a museum where objects from the city are kept, along with texts, curious items and illustrative graphs.

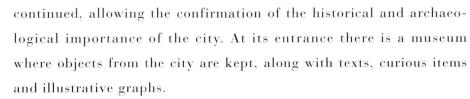

This prehispanic enclave abandoned about the year 900 A.D., is confined in three areas, the central or ceremonial that contains the richest buildings of religious and public character, apart from houses for the ruling class and the priests; a second ring contains the residences of lords and the farming areas with the homes of farmers and poor people. Space distribution is very important in Comalcalco, as squares, courtyards and important buildings maintain a correct orientation that is found in the core of their own beliefs.

The Great Acropolis, the Eastern Acropolis, still unexcavated, and the Northern Square are the three great architectural structures that can be seen in the city; the first is formed by a platform that is 35 m. high and on it sits a civic building called Palacio with terraces, squares and patios. On a lower space is found the tomb of the Nueve Señores de la Noche (Nine Lords of the Night), decorated with interesting stucco relieves and bearing great similarity with those of the tomb of the Inscriptions at Palenque. The Northern Square is a rectangular space consisting of a series of constructions and churches; it is oriented towards the cardinal points and its largest axis faces west, with three altars placed on it.

One of the more outstanding elements of the prehispanic city is that of the bricks used in its constructions, all in different sizes and decorations and various techniques such as incisions, relieves or paint. They were used in walls, altars, stairs or vaults, and on them appear hands, faces, important persons with luxurious dresses, animals, fantastic creatures, birds, fish or geometrical designs. Due to this, they represent an irreplaceable material to investigate the life and habits of Mayan culture.

Metztitlán

Deep in one of the most beautiful and impressive landscapes of the state of Hidalgo, Barranca de Metztitlán, lying next to a river that turns the neighboring lands in fertile treasures, there is a little town, that captivates at first sight and that gives its name to the ravine. The river, known by the same name as the town and the ravine, favors the presence of extraordinary farms of vegetables, cereals, and fruits, in addition to walnuts. The ravine, whose upper side rises 2.300 m above sea level, has a southeast-northeast orientation originating from two different origins, one next to Alcholoya and other near Apulco, both joining near the former town. As you get inside it, it becomes wider and deeper, and also, due to the presence of the river below, it creates two different landscapes in the same ravine; one is desert like with plants adapted to conditions of draughtness such as nopales, magueys or biznagas, in

Open gallery with wooden roof and columns on pedestals.

View of the town of Metztitlán, whose name means "Moonlit place".

47

the western section of the lower side, and other, very different, fertile and green on the bottom of the ravine. This ecosystem of Metztitlán was declared by decree in the year 2000 as reserve of the biosphere due to the rich natural heritage that remains here. The lagoon of Metztitlán can be found very near here, and is a place for recreation where it is possible to fish and ride.

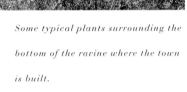

The culture known as Huasteca occupied, among many other areas, part of the state of Hidalgo, and its remains have been found in the neighboring areas. This territory was the home of otomíes, olmecas-xicallanga and tecpanecas, a fact which contributed to create an interesting cultural mixture, and traditions which show this multiple influence. The name of the town originates from the word náhuatl which means "Moonlit place", due to the fact that old warriors chose to fight on moonlit nights, and from their name, metzcas or metztitlonecas, comes the name of the town.

This beautiful town appears inside the landscape of the ravine and represents a small oasis of peace, very tempting after a trip through the surrounding area; in its picturesque streets the homes of its inhabitants have decorations that are typical of the area, and its main square performs as a social and amusement center. But, undoubtedly,

the most important building in Metztitlán is the convent erected by the Augustines around the middle of the XVI century and that was a priorate due to the importance of the place. Due to the conditions of the mountainous terrain, the builders had a complicated adaptation job, having leveled the ground to construct the convent and used a hill as a foundation. The work was started by brother Juan de Sevilla and protected by fortified construction, a common characteristic of that period. The church was built, first,

One of the walls of the convent that has suffered damages with the passing of time.

Characteristic square surrounded with buildings with arcades.

Some typical plants surrounding the bottom of the ravine where the town is built.

Plants and flowers in lively colors fill some of the walls in town.

48

and dedicated to the Santos Reyes, but a flood destroyed it a few years later and it had to be built and finished again in 1550. The church has large dimensions, oriented towards the east of the ravine, contains open chapels that were originally decorated with mural paintings and the atrium, also of large proportions, has an atrium cross. The façade of the church is in plateresque style, it has grooved columns and capitals and in the niches of the lower part it has images of St. Peter and Paul. The entablature bears a Latin inscription and on the upper part there is a sculpture of the Child God surrounded by angels; all the group is completed with a belfry of seven bays.

The interior of the church presents several objects, paintings and sculptures of interest, it is very high and is covered by ribbed and cannon vaults; there are good altarpieces of the XVII and XVIII centuries, but the most interesting one is the main altarpiece, finished at the end of the XVII century, that is unique in the country. The great local sculptor Salvador de Ocampo participated in the construction of this altarpiece dedicated to the Holy Kings.

Façade characterized by a half point arch supported by columns.

The valleys of this town have a melancholic aspect which gives them a special look.

Low reliefs, paintings and sculptures of great quality were made for this altarpiece and a complex iconographical program about the lives of the Virgin and Jesus was molded; there is a relief dedicated to the Adoration of the Magi, as well as sculptures of some famous members of the Augustinian Order, such as San Nicolás Tolentino and an image of the Eternal Father. Also, mural paintings were used to decorate the various sections of the convent, such as the refectory, the sacristy, cells, the hall of Profundis and the galleries;

An abandoned dwelling invaded by vegetation.

Another corner decorated with rose color flowers.

Façade of the magnificent convent whose church is dedicated to the Santos Reyes.

Details of remarkable mural
paintings preserved in the
Augustinian convents.

Interior design of the convent church
with the important main altarpiece

Pleasant image of the convent presided by the animal that can be seen in front.

the stairway to the floor above also presents a moralizing decoration intended for the residents of the convent with allegories to patience and sanctity.

This remarkable church is the stage for the solemn procession that takes place on Holy Friday during which those participating are dressed with black robes and hoods to walk through the town under candle lights and together with religious images. On the festivity of San Isidro Labrador, the 15th of May, a colorful celebration is held in this town, in honor of the farmer, which begins with the procession of the saint through the streets and farms and the celebration of an outdoor mass; for this purpose, crop offerings are made and farm animals and tractors are brought to be blessed. Afterwards, comes the meal shared and livened up with Huasteca typical music such as huapangos or sones huastecos. Between the 3rd and 10th of June, the town again celebrates with open air markets, dances, fireworks and exhibitions of agricultural products.

The landscapes surrounding this town are of incomparable beauty and are visited by sportsmen who practice outdoor activities.

Internal courtyard of the cloister, with escarzanos archs opening to it.

On the following page, a picture allows you to watch the beauty of the mural paintings in the convent.

Omitlán de Juárez

Located in one of the prettiest areas of the state of Hidalgo, surrounded by mountains and greenness, you can find this secluded municipality; it is a pleasure to walk its streets impregnated with a smell of the soil and plants. Close to this town there are interesting and beautiful natural spots such as Parque Nacional El Chico and small towns that retain the same charm and natural beauty as Omitlán de Juárez. This privileged natural enclave is common to many other parts of the state, and is one of its main attractions. The various forests, landscapes, cascades, deserts and lakes are distributed throughout the state and represent a valuable habitat for many species of animals and plants.

Its name originates from the terms *ome*, which means "number two", and *tlan*, short for tlantil , meaning "teeth", so that its name can be translated as "place of two teeth or molars". Its streets have

Stairs leading to the interior of the church, which has a high tower with horseshoe shaped arches.

Town square, with small arches in the central zone.

57

many picturesque details and some of its façades liven up with the typical bright colors that make you feel more cheerful when you watch them. One of the most beautiful spots of Omitlán de Juárez is its square, which is a required stop during a visit to this town; a fact that is enhanced by the presence of white benches strategically located for those walking by to sit on them, rest and observe the beautiful sight of the square and the town. Located between houses is an estate which is an example of local arquitecture, although the most interesting construction is the parish of El Refugio, a beautiful building with a high tower, remarkable for the disposition of its bodies, which decrease in size as they rise; the ground floor is shaped as a cross and the façade has elements of classic influence. The view of this church is very pretty and in front of its main façade there are trees planted to enrich the appearance of the whole group.

Some of the natural jewels of this town are Peña del Zumate, that can be reached through a forest, remarkable for its height. It is a rocky foundation which attracts many sportsmen who practice activities such as motocross, mountain biking or trekking; from it you can enjoy the extraordinary sights of the surrounding area. To enjoy the waters, there is also in this place a cascade, called Bandola, and a dam, that of Los Ángeles, where you can practice activities such as swimming, underwater diving, fishing or boating to enjoy the views.

One of the moments of the year most enjoyed by the inhabitants of Omitlán de Juárez and the visitors and travelers who visit it is the Feria de la Manzana (Apple Fair) that takes place on June 27 and July 6. It is considered the most important festivity of the town and during it are exhibited the best apples grown in the municipality. Some of the activities that take place during this fair are the election of the Queen of the

Town street decorated whit flags showing the Mexican colors.

Town kiosk surrounded by trees.

Interior of church whit simple decoration.

Façade whit balconies and small wooden roofs.

In this town you can find many facades painted in lively colors.

Apple, typical dances where you can see samples of the traditional folklore of the state of Hidalgo, bullfights, and an exhibition of beautiful handicrafts made by the local people. Another important festivity is that of the Virgen del Refugio, held on July 4, although celebrations last for several days, including cultural and sporting events, gastronomic fairs where you can enjoy typical local dishes and the popular antojitos, fireworks and display of local handicrafts. The biggest attraction of this town, its natural beauty and that of its surrounding area, is demonstrated by the activities displayed by the local people, such as rose growing, producing samples which are very attractive, with petals like velvet, renowned for their beauty.

House in Omitlán de Juarez next to a cobbled street.

Porch covered with wooden roof.

Xilitla

An extraordinary feeling covers you from the first moment in a dreamy atmosphere, with surrealist corners that carry you to other corners where magic, sub conscience and the unbelievable are the guidelines that rule the atmosphere. All the incredible objects that exist in this place play leading parts in surprising and different stories that are whispered by the wind filtering among the stones of this construction known by the original artist, El Castillo, which is undoubtedly one of the most troubling, captivating and incredible spots in Mexico. This marvel is found in Xilitla, a pleasant population located in the Sierra Madre, surrounded by tropical vegetation and clean water currents. This area of the Huasteca Potosina is known by the presence of deep caves, which attract the lovers of adventure and potholing such as Hoya de la Luz and Salitre. In their interior stalactites have formed curious shapes, called because of their shape, El Gigante or La

The streets of this town are quiet places where the life of its people goes by.

Houses of Xilitla, many of them protected by roof.

63

bruja; inside them it is possible to watch a large number of parakeets or parvadas starting their flight.

All the beauties of Xilitla make it an unbelievable place among the hills on the slope of a high mountain from which you can see the deep ravine at the bottom of which is the riverbed of the Tanculín river. Its name means "place of snails" and the inhabitants exhibit lots of charm and humor, especially during the social gathering in the square. Its steep alleys are full of the typical flavor of local architecture; one of the most remarkable buildings is the Franciscan convent built early in the XVI century, which suffered serious damage due to an attack in the last quarter of the century. It was a large building built in a sturdy fashion, with the usual characteristics of a temple-fortress, and across a big square used by the residents for different purposes. Because of the fortress built therein it resembled a military construction more than a

religious one. Its high walls were covered by a patting of moss, a consequence of age and one which lends it a mysterious air: Festivities in this town take place on September 28th in honor of La Soledad, on August 27th, St. Augustine's Day, during the first fifteen days of May, when the fair and cock fights take place, and on the 15th of November, when the regional fair begins.

Xilitla had a rotund impact on an interesting person named Edward James, the creator of the building and complex known as El Castillo. He was originally from Great Britain, a descendant of Edward VII of England, owner of a great wealth and an artist who was associated to the surrealist movement and to its participants, having supported many unknown youngsters and having received visits from the likes of Picasso, Dalí or Stravinsky. James visited Mexico originally thanks to the invitation of the writer Huxley in order to see Cuernavaca. The artist found it to be too crowded with tourist and decided to find a place deep in the country, with the help of a guide called Gastélum. He built himself a house on the outskirts of town, where his companion lived and watched El Castillo. When they reached Xilitla the appearance of many butterflies was interpreted by James as a sign, and he decided to stay in this place and build a house next to the cascades and oasis that existed there.

The estate was designed by Gastélum, following instructions from the artist, and its construction extended throughout the second half of the XX century, remaining unfinished. The architecture borrows from the shape of trees, plants and nature and the latter appears to harmonize perfectly in the surroundings imitating the architectural structures such as the large tree trunks that resemble columns of stone. Architecture and nature join to form an indivisible world crowded with staircases, ramps, paths, terraces, bridges, solitary spots, lights and shadows.

Another street in town with the Augustinian convent in the background.

There are sculptures everywhere with shapes like snakes, so common in the Mexican culture, as well as suns of stone, huge flowers, plants and surrealistic images, among which can be found animals of different species. One of the most attractive places is the one formed by the cascade and the oasis where the water rest, which is called Las Pozas, a place frequently visited by the artist when he lived in Xilitla and a favorite of the local inhabitants for a day of relaxation.

Today this estate features a spa and guest rooms. It was the home of Edward James and his family for many years, having left the luxuries of England for this Mexican paradise. The artists spent his time, in the seclusion of El Castillo, reading or writing, and he enjoyed specially the facilities around Las Pozas.

Windows of a house protected by grillwork and a balcony above.

The devotion of the population does not need great means of expression, needing only flowers and candles.

The picture shows an excellent sample of iron grill.

Calvillo

There is a legend in the State of Aguascalientes that tells about splendid lands in its territory and the prosperity of its crops. This story may have been started in Calvillo, a town surrounded by beautiful landscapes, with large areas planted with guava that give off a delicious smell within its corners and offers the beneficial effect of thermal waters in its spas. Located at 50 km of the capital of the state, on the valley of Huejúcar and nest to the Calvillo river, it offers travelers beautiful and quiet places where to enjoy nature. In this area it is farmed a tree called *xacalasúchil*, a rare species that produces a very valuable rubber.

The interior of the church of Calvillo is surprising for its beauty and a careful polychromatic decoration on its walls and coverings.

When, at the middle of the XVI century, the Spaniards arrived at these lands, they found in them Nagua residents and they gave them the name El Salitre or El Salitrillo. Later, during the early years of the XVIII century and thanks to the good farmland of the area, the village

Town street, showing pavement with cobblestones.

71

was growing and became a town. In 1771, by decree of the governor of the Mitra in Guadalajara, the parish of San José de Huejúcar was established, with a name meaning "place of Willows" and the district of this valley was declared village. The area had belonged to José Calvillo, owner of the San Nicolás estate, and later donated as a location for the town. For this reason the municipal council adopted his surname as name for the town.

Details of the remarkable cave mural paintings that can be admired near Calvillo.

Beautiful shrine topped by a balustrade

In its main square, it is possible to find a curious trail of the independence route, formed by an eagle. In early ages it was completely planted with orange trees and was built in the last quarter of the XVIII century. Next to it there are buildings such as the Municipal House, los portales and the church. To the same period belongs the church of the Señor del Salitre, in whose interior there is an important collection of paintings and it is also worth mentioning the well-known church of Guadalupe. Another place that can be

The church of Calvillo, which offers a rotund and forceful aspect.

On the following page, an entrance with a roof and balcony above.

Details of the superb decoration showing the coverings of the Calvillo church.

On the following page, a bust and an inscription relative to the priest Hidalgo.

visited is the house where Miguel Hidalgo lived on his way north from Guadalajara.

The region where Calvillo is located is rich in historical and natural attractions; for lovers of potholing, there can be found in this municipality the caves of La Barranca, El Toro, El Pastor, and Gruta de los Murciélagos, where you can find marvelous formations. Also there are resorts for climbers, as in one of the extensions of the cold sierra, Sierra del Laurel, there are marvelous rocky foundations of basaltic type that would delight the lovers of this sport. Water sports and fishing have their spot at the Malpaso dam, which is surrounded by beautiful areas, ideal for resting; of similar beauty are the Codorniz dam where you can have delicious seafood and fish dishes, and the cascade of Huenchos. You can also enjoy the water at the spas found in this municipality, such as La Palma and Ojo Caliente. As if this was not enough, you can also find in Calvillo the extraordinary cave paintings of El Tepozán, which show anthropomorphic polychromatic figures.

The typical dish in this town is birria de carneto, the breads called canelitas and, of course, a great variety of desserts based on guava, such as empanadas, guava in syrup and guayabate, not forgetting jamoncillos de leche and charrascas. As for beverages, the vino de membrillo and agua de pingüica are a must. The skilful hands of its inhabitants also manufacture remarkable objects of craftsmanship such as the famous openwork embroidery, always present at the Feria Nacional de San Marcos. Another important fair for the township is that of La Guayaba, held between the 3rd and 12th of December, the festivities are held in January in honor of the

A street in town, seen from behind a grille.

One of the most quiet corners in Calvillo is this garden, its beauty enhanced by flowers and a fountain.

On the following page, *details of an urn where an image of Christ wearing a long gown is preserved.*

Wide open gallery where streets stands are established.

The extreme simplicity of this religious construction is noticeable.

The dam in this picture is surrounded by a beautiful landscape and is one of the attractions of this area.

Inmaculate Conception and San Diego de la Labor, in July for Virgen del Refugio, in November La Medallita Milagrosa and the Patron Saint which is held on Ascension Thursday in Honor of Señor del Salitre. During these festivities many shows take place such as dances of matachines, bullfights, sport activities, parades and games.

Near Calvillo there are other typical towns worthy of a visit, such as La Panadera, where beautiful embroideries are made, the town of Ojocaliente y Malpaso, a town of cobbled streets surrounded by refreshing plants such as the lemon and orange trees, that has a beautiful church dedicated to the Virgen del Refugio.

Tequila

The interior of the church has a peculiar system of lighting consisting of many small bulbs.

T he name of this municipality is that of a very special product that is always identified with Mexico, known worldwide and rooted in the legendary and historic tradition of the various cultures which inhabited the country namely tequila, a drink obtained from maguey and that is basically prepared in this region of the State of Jalisco. In it, in the place called Teochinchán, lived the chichimecas, toltecas and náhuatls, and for the latter the maguey had a divine origin, and represented the goddess *Mayáuel* who had 400 breasts to feed the same number of children; she was married to the god *Petácatl*, protector of several plants which participate in the fermentation of pulque, a drink used in ceremonies and special occasions. Its leaves were also used to manufacture clothes, ropes, paper, poultices and medicines, apart from been used as covers in the houses, for these reasons this vegetable was

Each house in Tequila has an unique peculiarity which distinguishes it from the rest, without breaking the armony of its streets.

On the foreground, a famous blue
used to prepare the world renowned
tequila.

Façade of the church of La Purísima,
constructed in stone and columns
that surround its bays.

considered as something magic and sacred and respected by the
ancient dwellers.

In 1530 the conquerors founded a town at the spot where Tequila
raises today, and it promptly gained importance and headed a rectification of the New Kingdom of Galicia; in 1824 a decree gave this
town the denomination of municipality and in 1874 it was raised to
the rank of city. Also, this famous name gives its name to the valley
where the municipality is established and of the dormant volcano on
whose slopes grows the valuable blue agave, from which tequila is
obtained, a name derived from a náhuatl term meaning "cutting
place". The outskirts of this town have beautiful enclaves that can
be visited, such as the cascades La Toma and Los Azules that form
quiet natural pools, the spas or the road ordered by emperor
Maximilian of Habsburg.

Details of window protected by
grillwork showing some decorations.

Also, the buildings and corners of tequila merit a leisure visit that
could start across the entrance to the church of La Purísima, built
in stone with a two-body façade. On the lower one there is a half
point arch and a medallion, while the upper one has a vegetable
decoration, padding and a window between columns. In memory
of the place where a cross was found among the brushwood, a
chapel was erected with the name Santa Cruz de los Espinos, and
another chapel, that of El Calvario, was built over the ruins of a
previous church dedicated to the Señor de los Desamparados. Quinta
Sauza was dedicated to the production of tequila and it houses a
museum at present; worth mentioning are its garden decorated
with fountains and sculptures and the corridors with high reliefs.

Ornamental barrels with woodcuts
containing tequila.

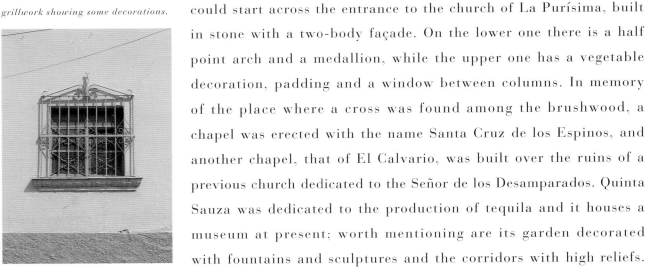

In this street you can see an
ornamental fountain made with
colorful tiles forming geometrical
figures.

Beautiful corner of a house with
interior garden and a gallery with a
portico which opens towards it.

Other decorative fountain in Tequila, with benches surrounding it.

In this town, as could be expected, there are many enterprises engaged in the production and marketing of tequila.

In 1888 in this farm was obtained the first production of tequila for export. The tequila factories are a required stop during the walk through the town and we would be surprised to watch the process followed by the plant to become the valuable drink.

Many are the festivities celebrated by the citizens of Tequila, one of which answers to the devotion to Santa Cruz de los Espinos and is held between the first and third of May with dances, food and drink; during the festivities of San Juan Bautista, San Pedro y San Pablo and the Patron Saint, it is common to see cantaritos, pitchers of baked clay cut in the outskirts of town and which are very popular. As could be expected Tequila is rooted in the popular culture of this place and plays a leading role in one of the best known festivities, the Tequila National Fair, held during early December and during which you can happily enjoy the music of mariachis, fireworks, cock fights and typical meals which include this drink. These gastronomic jewels are pozole, enchiladas and birria. Also in this town are manufactured colorful craft items such as the small barrels made of oak, commonly named palo colorado, decorated with images relative to the tequila. Also there are containers covered with pigskin that have inscriptions relative to popular phrases and sayings and used as the case of the barrels to contain tequila.

Since the pre-Columbian period, maguey has been appreciated for its many properties, having been called "árbol de las maravillas" (tree of marvels) in the XVI century by Joseph de Acosta; maybe this is the reason that these plants, with 200 different species received the name agave, which means marvel in Greek. At the beginning of the XX century a European biologist, Dr. Weber,

Monument commemorating the important work of the tequila producer and the importance of this beverage to the town.

Open air market, where you can buy different products.

published a lengthy study about the blue agave, proposing the name of *agave tequilana*, and since then, it is known, in his honor, *agave tequilana Weber azul*. The first news about the preparation of tequila originate in the first half of the XVII century, when after the introduction of methods and techniques needed for the process of consumption of mescal were spreading at the beginning of the XVII century agave went from growing wild to been harvested in the tequila region, which had all the necessary water to prepare the drink and in this place was established the first tavern, adequately equip-

Kiosk of tequila formed by a based painted in two colors and a complex forged worked on the upper part.

One of the places where tequila is manufactured since the XIX century.

The doors on this façade are very simple and have mouldings above them.

ped, which was followed by others, thus this area becoming a fundamental point of preparation and distribution of tequila throughout the country.

Preparation of the drink begins with the cutting of plants that later are introduced in the sterilizing unit where they are submitted to a boiling process during four hours at a temperature of 105 °C. This cooked product will then pass to a machine that will grind it and afterwards to a mill that will extract the mescal juice injecting water to facilitate the operation; the residual matter after extracting all the juice is called bagazo. Fermentation takes place in jars to which are added yeast and juices and will remain during 72 hours, after

which the product goes to distillation towers and then stored in a tank, a result of the first distillation known as Ordinario; then the rectification column will be responsible for obtaining tequila, which will be stored in different types of barrels, where they remain for different periods depending on the kind of tequila desired. Before passing to the process of bottling and labeling the product will be diluted with distilled water in order to obtain the desired alcoholic proof.

These stairs lead to the upper floor with a pretty grille decorated with geometrical designs.

Yuriria

In the early years of the XVI century a construction work was started of various convents promoted by different religious orders that arrived in Mexico, such as Augustinians, Franciscans or Dominicans; these constructions have stood throughout the centuries and represent one of the most important artistic treasures, where local elements and imported concepts are blended in harmony. One of the states where numerous convents are preserved is Guanajuato, where the town of Yuriria is located, and where the most famous convent of the State, San Pablo de Yuririapúndaro is situated.

The territory where this town is today was populated during prehispanic time by the Tarascos, and its name in purépecha is *Yuririapúndaro*, which means "blood lagoon". In the second quarter of the XVI century, the Augustine Order, led by brother Diego de Chávez y Alvarado, founded the capital of the municipality, and construction began

89

Corner of Yuriria with the group of church bells in the background.

of buildings that later constituted the framework of the town and the remarkable convent, began around 1540; in July, 1852 it was declared a village by decree. In its coat of arms, there appear three trunks of ahuehuete, of great historic significance for the population, and a circle that represents the rock from which a spring flows.

Yuriria rests in the side of a precious artificial lagoon of the same name, developed in the middle of the XVI century by brother Diego de Chávez in order to communicate the Lerma River, changing the course of part of its waters with a stream. Its maximum width is 7 km, measuring 17 km from East to West, and in it there are several islands that can be visited to enjoy their beauty. This lagoon also receives waters from the Cuitzeo Lake, through the Moroleón River, which forms the dam of Huahuemba. The surrounding area is mountainous, there are volcanic materials and some of the most important elevations are Cerro Grande, Colorado, Santiago, El Varal, Los Amoles o El Porullo, with an average height of 2.300 m over sea level, located on the North side of the lagoon. In the arable lands, it is possible to find wheat, corn, barley, tunas, frijol, guava and durazno, fundamental ingredients of delicious typical dishes, such as *xoconoxtles* salad or tamales of chickpeas, the baked fruits and charamuscas. The craftsmanship articles found in this place are

At Yuriria, you can see beautiful old buildings with remarkable architectural elements, such as the one in the picture.

Picture taken from inside a building which allows you to watch the surrounding landscape and lagoon.

Several businesses in town, painted in attractive colors.

Other street in town, with its

colorful stores.

Façade with an interesting

decorative frieze and sculptural

lamps on the bays.

Beautiful view of the Yuriria lagoon,

surrounded by mountains and

grazing fields.

Fragment of the kiosk and the impressive façade of the San Pablo convent.

ceramic objects, wax figures, embroideries, textiles, wicker and silver jewels. Other samples of the popular culture are the dances, such as that of the Moorish and Christians of old folks, club bearers or shepherds, staged during the Yuriria festivities, the most important of which are the Festival de la Preciosa Sangre de Cristo (Precious Blood of Christ), 3rd of January and Carnival Sunday.

Yuriria has areas of great beauty, such as parks and gardens, its streets of small houses, and some family textile workshop, but undoubtedly the main interest lies in the magnificent Augustine Convent, of plateresque style, surrounded by a great open space that reinforces, if possible, its walls; this area is used by the inhabitants as a social gathering place and also for festivities. The area formed by the convent buildings and the church was built hastily in nine or ten years, under the direction of brother Diego de Chávez and the project made by the Spanish architect Pedro del Toro; its inauguration took place on a Thursday, Corpus Christi Day, with all due solemnity. The church has one of the most decorated places, the main façade has three bodies, an exceptional jewel where plateresque motifs crowd the surface, and you can notice the hand of local

One of the magnificent mural paintings which are kept in the convent of San Pablo.

94

Gallery, opening to the courtyard in

the convent of Yuriria, which shows

pictorial decoration, grooved

columns and starred vaults.

Municipal palace façade, across a

small garden.

artists. The other façade, on the side, is also in plateresque style although it is no as magnificent. Of the great external front it is worth mentioning the tower formed by three bodies.

The ground floor of the church has the shape of a Latin cross and the nave is covered by a cannon vault decorated with casetones while the transfer and the presbytery are covered with ribbed vaults. In one of the internal corners there is a place for the devotion and affection of the people of Yuriria; it is an altar dedicated to brother Miguel Zavala, died in 1947, next to it, in one of the sides of the presbytery, stands the chapel of the Beato, dedicated to Bartolomé Gutiérrez, a priest who left in the early days of the XVII century going to the Philippine Islands in an Evangelization Mission and later traveled to Japan where he died in 1632; in 1867 he was beatified by Pope Pious IX.

On the right side of the church stands the convent, which can be entered through a four arch portico, once inside you rich a hall that shows the access to the museum, formed by four halls where religious sculptures and paintings of the XVII and XVIII centuries can be seen, aside from numerous objects of the prehispanic and colonial periods. It is interesting to watch the renaissance-style cloister, formed by arches over grooved columns and galleries covered with gothic and cannon shaped vaults that retain remains of mural paintings of religious nature. In the courtyard there is a kerb of a well among plants and fruit trees and to gain access to the higher floor there is a great staircase covered with grooved vaults, the cells opened in the upper cloister still preserve a sober atmosphere of past centuries and it is possible to find in them objects used in monks daily life.

Tzintzuntzán

T his town awakens among the mist and the shreds of clouds that seem to mingle above the quiet waters of Lake Pátzcuaro, in whose banks seats this town of unforgettable name, and which, in spite of its simple and accessible aspect, was in other era the capital of the great Tabasco Empire and one of the most important cities of western Mexico. Its name originates from a word that in náhuatl means "place with many hummingbirds" although other meanings have been given to it such as "place of the mensajero hummigbird" or even the onomatopoeia of the sound the bird makes during flight. The great importance given by the Tabasco people to the hummingbird was due to the fact that it represents one of the its most important gods, *Huitzilopochtli*, who led them in their pilgrimage towards the South and that even one of its gods took the name *Tzintzuni*, or hummingbird.

View of the town, with its characteristic cobbled streets.

As it is very common in Mexico, some façades have arcades built with wood and painted in different colors.

101

It became capital after *Tariácuri* divided the kingdom among his relatives, his nephew *Tangaxhuan* inheriting the territory of Tzintzuntzán. After the death of *Tariácuri*, his nephew succeeded him and installed it as capital of the kingdom. He shared this title with Pátzcuaro, as cultural and spiritual center, and with Qurínguaro, which was the place where economic and administrative matters were centralized. In *Relaciones de Michoacán* was described that these three capitals of the empire had a bird and a color to differentiate them. The one of Tzintzuntzán had the green color of the feathers of the hummingbird, Pázcuaro has the white of the heron feathers and Quirínguaro the red color of the macaws of Michoacán; these colors appear in the Mexican flag.

The sharp contrast of the houses of this town in noticeable; with its white washed walls and divided roofs of red tiles; among the houses appears the magnificent convent built by the initiative of the Franciscan Order in the XVI century. This construction has a great atrium and olives that were planted, according to history, by Vasco de Quiroga, known as Tata Vasco. Brother Pedro de Pila started the building of this convent that has a remarkable dome and a font built near open-air altars. Inside the church there are frescoes and images of many saints that are object of devotion by the people, such as San Miguel Arcángel, St. Peter and St. Paul, the Virgen del Carmen and the Dolorosa.

One of the most interesting festivities of Tzintzuntzán is the one of Día de Difuntos, with a surprising procession that travels the side of Lake Pátzcuaro, illuminating it with the lights of many candles and finishing at the cemetery where a vigil is kept during all night for the souls of the dead. During the day there are dances and songs such as *Los viejitos de Jarácuaro*, *Los guerreros* or *El pescado de Janitzio*. During the month of February takes place the festivity of Señor del Rescate, an image that was kept by the Franciscans in their convent and which is carried on that day to the altar in the church of San Francisco. To complete this traditional popular

manifestation there are an open market and a pilgrimage during which the most typical and delicious dishes of the local gastronomy are enjoyed, such as churipo, a kind of pozole with vegetables and beef, and the uchepos, tamales of sweet elote. Other dishes that can be enjoyed are tamales tarascos, mole michoacano, caldo de charazes, pollo entamalado and the delicious white fish from Lake Pátzcuaro, famous in the whole country. The most delicious desserts are ates morelianos, alfajor de coco, dulce de leche and chongos zamoranos.

An important witness of this mythical past of the area of Tzintzuntzán is the archeological zone of Las Yácatas; the city was placed on a hill and was divided in various residential areas inhabited by different social classes: a big terrace with walls was built to support the construction. In its center there were religious and social buildings, and this area is what is known today as archeological zone which bore the name *Tariaran*, according

to the *Relaciones de Michoacán*, meaning "house of wind", around it there were houses, workshops and small temples. In the central area five T shaped pyramids were built which were called Yácatas and that have a circular inner core. They were dedicated to the solar god of the Tarasco people *Curicaheri* and his four brothers, although they could represent the five arrows thrust by king *Uacús* in the hill where the pyramids rise. Above them were built wooden temples used to carry out ritual celebrations, ceremonies and government events; inside them remains of burials of the higher classes were found. One of the bigger constructions in the city is the so-called Palacio that has several rooms used by the priests. In it human remains have been found, such as perforated skulls, which probably belonged to their enemies. There are also altars, buildings from later eras and warehouses. In the Museum of the area it is possible to see samples coming from the city and in this place the history of its existence is explained.

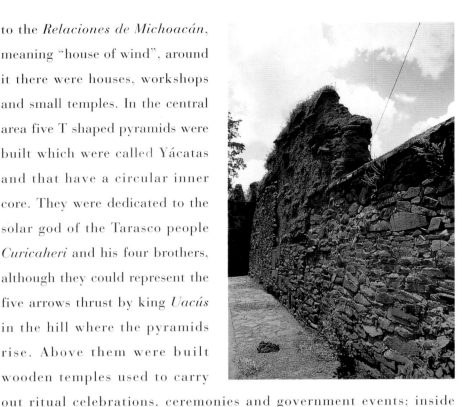

Many remains of constructions which remain and were built at the time Vasco de Quiroga arrived in Tzintzuntzán.

The works of art produced by the local people with their hands and with a lot of patience are varied, but, perhaps one of the best known is the work made with straw, such as numerous figures and vases, ships, religious images or baskets, all made of wet straw to prevent it from breaking. Pieces of pottery are also very beautiful, decorated with figures of fishermen, fish and ducks, all inspired by the presence of the peaceful Lake Pátzcuaro.

Simple corner displaying a remarkable religious painting.

Entrance formed by half point arch supported by pilasters.

Pátzcuaro

MICHOACÁN

T he name Pátzcuaro reminds you of a magnificent past lived by Purépechas, with beautiful colonial jewels, courtyards full of multicolored flowers and a sheet of water with enigmatic islands full of color. Around the year 1.000 A.D., an alliance of the peoples who lived in this area and the Chichimecas gave birth to the Purépecha culture, which selected Pátzcuaro as a sacred city, as they thought was the place through which the gods entered and made their exit; its name in Purépecha means "Asiento de templos" (Seat of temples) or "where the stone is which indicates the access to paradise" and its ceremonial center was located on a slope.

The city was founded around the year 1.300 and soon gained great importance; the arrival of bishop Vasco de Quiroga in the second quarter of the XVI century took Pátzcuaro through a second period of splendor, becoming in the headquarters of the diocese and initiating a

Pátzcuaro Lake , with some of the

islands and high mountains in the

background.

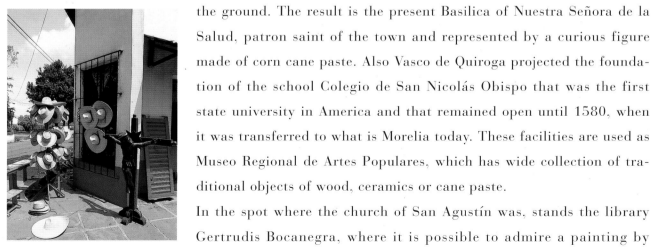

constructive period that left behind churches, schools, squares and homes that are kept today. Vasco de Quiroga wanted to build a big cathedral with a floor in the shape of an open hand, an ambitious project for the period that couldn't be finished because of problems of the ground. The result is the present Basilica of Nuestra Señora de la Salud, patron saint of the town and represented by a curious figure made of corn cane paste. Also Vasco de Quiroga projected the foundation of the school Colegio de San Nicolás Obispo that was the first state university in America and that remained open until 1580, when it was transferred to what is Morelia today. These facilities are used as Museo Regional de Artes Populares, which has wide collection of traditional objects of wood, ceramics or cane paste.

In the spot where the church of San Agustín was, stands the library Gertrudis Bocanegra, where it is possible to admire a painting by

Juan O'Gorman dedicated to the history of the Purepecha people. The church and school of Compañía de Jesús were planned in the XVI century although work started in the middle of the following century; the complex houses the Casa de Cultura. The best kept tradition of the people of Pátzcuaro points out that the oldest church in town is the Hospitalito, distinguished by its façade finished in the XVI century; other façade worth mentioning, of baroque style, is that of the church and hospital of San Juan de Dios, constructed in the XVII century. Pátzcuaro is full of churches and chapels, all of them built by wise hands that created beautiful shapes in the styles of the period and the local traditions. Some of these constructions are the church of San Francisco, with a façade in renaissance style, the chapel of El Calvario, built in the second half of the XVII century above the tomb of the Purépecha king Tariácuri, or El Sagrario, previously named Nuestra Señora de la Salud, built at the end of the XVI century.

The historic trajectory and past splendor of Pátzcuaro can be felt in many of

Beginning of a remarkable set of arches over fluted columns.

the rich and joyful homes built centuries ago but retaining admirable treasures which surprise the visitors; the Palace of Huitziméngari, built for the son of king Tangaxhuán II, has a patio of great beauty. La Casa de los Once Patios (the house with eleven courtyards) was a convent of Dominican nuns built in the middle of the XVIII century and used today as trading point for the beautiful handicrafts of this area, and is famous in all the State of Michoacán. La Casa del Gigante (house of giant) that belonged to the counts of Menocal, receives this name because of a large sculpture of a soldier with his hand on the hilt of a sword, which is placed in the upper part of the starcase. Around the main square there are remarkable houses such as the Portal Chaparro, with arches lower than those of the rest of the buildings, Casa de los Escudos (house of shields) with the arms of Condes de Villahermosa

Remarkable inside of the church, decorated with paintings, stuccos and gilts.

Another corner of town, formed by a sloping street.

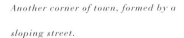

Busy town street, dominated by the façade of the church.

114

Building with porches of wood and
stones.

Façade of stone, painted and with
several stores.

Interior look of one of the best
known buildings in town, the so
called Casa de los Once Patios.

de Alfaro on the façade, or Casa de los Venicia, with baroque decorations in its balconies.

In spite of the indescribable feeling that the town provokes when you cross it, the corners having the most charming atmosphere, the intoxicating feeling of being at the heart of it all, are the squares and patios of the homes of the people of Pátzcuaro, and specially, the main square dedicated to Vasco de Quiroga, considered one of the most beautiful in Mexico, which is surrounded by many noble homes built during colonial times. In its center the statue of the bishop, known by the friendly name of Tata Vasco. Other squares worthy of a mention are those of San Francisco and Gertrudis Bocanegra, also presided by an sculpture which represents this heroine. Even more attractive are the patios, which are maintained and decorated untiringly by the owners and where it is possible to find countless types of flowers,

118

Interior court and galleries with stone arches which ornamented keystones.

with the begonia as the most characteristic of this town. The smell and colors of the flowers are framed in a traditional architecture typical of these houses, some of which were built in the XVII century and combine with fountains decorated with mosaics.

Another typical color, similar to those of the flowers, can be enjoyed during the popular festivities which take place on June 24th day of St. John the Baptist, the Corpus Christi, October 4th, St. Francis of Assisi's Day, and the Day of the Deceased. It is necessary that you find time to watch these celebrations during which traditional activities take place.

The gastronomy of Pátzcuaro offers delightful variety of dishes, many of them based on fish from the lake, such as the famous white fish, charales, acúmura or mojarra. Also delicious are the different kind of tamales such as uchepos, sopa tarasca, chocolate casero (homemade chocolate) and the ice creams.

Another beautiful corner of this town where we can find places of great beauty.

The doors of this façade are highlighted by stone frames.

Interior court with plants and balconies with standing out grilles.

Xochimilco

An impossible dream, materialized and alive for many centuries, a Herculean breath capable of defying nature and modify its surroundings with techniques that were amazing for the period when they were put to use an oasis in the center of a great city immersed in the daily routine and speed, that is Xochimilco, a territory with lakes inherited from Tenochtitlán, where the veils of history have been settling since the pre-Columbian peoples and whose name means "place of flowers".

The former dwellers knew how to take advantage of the condition of the lagoons and invented a system to make these extensive zones arable, that otherwise would not have been usable. The water were shallow, with much vegetation where the spaces were marked with stakes and the ditches were filled with mud from the same lagoon; over these marks, were placed the chinampas, floating formations

Colorful trajineras which bear female names in front.

Canals with extensive recreation areas.

123

On the following page, *façade of the church of San Bernardino Xochimilco.*

made with roots, and stalks of zacatón, chichicastle or lirio (lilies) that receives the name *atlapalácatl*. The name *chinampa* comes from a *chinamitl* word meaning "hedges of canes". The remaining spaces were filled with mud, to form a stable surface next to which trees were planted such as ahuejotes and sabinos, a species with large roots that hold the chinampas and leaves that allow the passing of sunrays and air. These formations

Details of some of the species growing in Xochimilco.

are excellent for the crops because of the high humidity and become truly floating gardens containing multicolored flowers and many agricultural products. The first inhabitants of the valley who built the system used the water from rivers and spring, which originated in that area and made possible the flow of water among the chinampas.

Soon an inhospitable territory where it was not possible to live or cross, started to become a place full of plantations, meeting places,

Due to the special climatic conditions in the area, there is a wide variety of plants.

One of the canals, between Chinampas and Ahuejotes.

and of transit to other zones and that even supported daily life in the houses built on the areas were the ground had reached firmness. It was a testimony of the greatness of these peoples that they transformed nature through the creation of systems and techniques that were very advanced. The canals and apantles (narrower canals) were used to move from one place to another in canoes, which docked on the edges of the chinampas where they put stones to preserve them in a better way. Nowadays these same waterways used by the original farmers can be made in boats known as trajineras, which are painted in vivid colors, decorated with flowers and have their name written on the front or side, usually a feminine one. This system of chinampas was used in other territories such as the Texcoco lake, and in them were constructed the homes, a

Small altar with the image of the Virgin surrounded by flowers.

Street of Xochimilco, with homes and
stores.

Details of an odd fountain formed by
ceramic containers.

Some of the flowers planted in
avenues and flowerbeds.

normal practice until 1940, when the traditional habits began to change. The period of maximum splendor of the chinampas took place between the XV and XVII centuries; already during the XVI century this system was gradually disappearing due to the use of farms on solid ground. At the beginning of the XX century new impulse was given to the chinampa farms, trying to recover the tradition of the valley of Mexico.

To enjoy a trip by trajinera through the canals of Xochimilco is an unforgettable experience; apart from the vegetation, flowers and farms it is possible to see the neighborhoods and the most beautiful constructions. The San Bernardino de Siena church was begun in 1535, in a place where there had been another religious construction

Although it may be a simple corner,
flags and decorations with Mexican
colors are always present.

In Xochimilco there are many pretty
and friendly places where to walk.

The phrase seen in the picture reflects the devotion and love of the people towards the Niñopan.

On the following page, entrance to the Ecological Park of Xochimilco.

Some buildings are located on the edges of canals, surrounded by vegetation.

built with perishable materials. At first, the nave was covered with a wooden roof that was replaced in the XVIII century by a vault and an octagonal dome. Inside it there are beautiful altarpieces, constructed between the XVI and XVIII centuries; some of the most outstanding are that of the Virgin of Guadalupe, which as a XVI century image of Saint Sebastian, and the main altarpieces, in plateresque style. The convent was built in the last quarter of the XVI century, with two stories and mural paintings, of which fragments are preserved and the whole complex was worthy renaissance and plateresque façades. Some of the chapels that are worth visiting are the one of Xaltocán, that has an XVIII century altarpiece and a baroque front, the chapel of the San Pedro neighborhood, which is one of the vice regal period as it was built in 1530 and today is dedicated to Saint Peter (San Pedro Apóstol), or the chapel of Rosario, with a magnificent stucco façade that resembles a filigree. From the higher part of Xochimilco it is possible to see the canals and the urban complex, and specially different religious constructions such as the parish of San Francisco Tlanepantla or the quiet chapels spread throughout the town.

Apart from the religious buildings, it is possible to enjoy in Xochimilco the homes of its inhabitants, that always have a distinguishing characteristic, or the Museum Dolores Olmedo, located in the old estate of Noria and home to the

Public open air bar with tables protected by sunshades.

most important collection of the painter Diego Rivera, apart from works of Frida Kalho, traditional Mexican and prehispanic pieces. The most boisterous moment takes place when the market, one of the most visited of the zone, opens. Uncountable craftsmanship products, agricultural, food and clothing, and also flowers and plants that make it famous, are sold.

If the structure of canals and chinampas picks up the echo of the prehispanic traditions, in the festivities and celebrations of Xochimilco is present the religious and popular life of its primitive settlers. One of the most beloved and respected figures is the Niñopan or Santo Niño del Pueblo, a name originating from náhuatl and meaning "Child of the Place", to whom several miracles are attributed and is present in many religious ceremonies, specially at Christmas. It does not have a church because it belongs to the whole town and passes through the streets so that the people can make their requests. The Niñopan is also present in April 30th, the Día del Niño, and at Corpus Christi, when they dress it in traditional clothes.

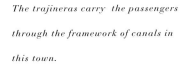

Ixtapan del Oro

Located in the center of exuberant mountain greenness, sieved by the mist and witness to crystal clear cascades, abandoned gold mines and prehistoric remains that demonstrate their past, is the town of Ixtapan del Oro, a special place since the times of the original Indian dwellers. This importance is explained by the meaning of its name, which comes from the Aztec word *ixtapan* that means "place of salt or on salt" and for the existence of important gold deposits mined during the XIX century. The first settlements in this zone, particularly in the Tepalcate Hill, were made by Tolteca groups, although also the Tarasca or Matlazinca influence left their marks; for these prehispanic dwellers salt was one of the most valued and luxurious elements and there was even a ritual for its purification.

The rich mines that attracted a great number of people in search of fortune and favored an important commercial activity in the XIX century

Church of Ixtapan del Oro, with its characteristic whitewashed walls and its high five bodied tower.

One of the cobbled streets of this town, with its façades and house roofs.

can still be seen around this town and some of them present beautiful formations of stalagmites and stalactites. Also nearby is the architectural zone of El Pedregal, with important prehispanic remains and where was found the curious sculpture that can be seen today in the main square next to the kiosk. This monolith represents a snake from whose open jaws comes out a figure with a skin on its face, probably a priest with a victim's skin; a representation is linked to the Quetzalcóatl pyramid in Teotihuacán and its myth. The kiosk was built in the XIX century, having an octagonal body, a stone base, and wooden columns and over them a roof of red tiles contrasting with the happy colors of the flowers and plants that decorate the beautiful garden of the square.

Across the street is located the church dedicated to San Martin Ocoxochitepec, constructed in the XVII century with an open atrium and entrance with an arch of half point and pyramidal top; are noticeable in this construction the grills and the clock tower which has five sides and is topped by a dome. The Municipal Palace is another building worth describing with its floors of black earthenware and onyx. To complete the visit to this town it is necessary to see the former farm of Tutuapilla where the poet Joaquín Arcadio Pagaza, who authored poems dedicated to this town, lived.

In the pretty streets of Ixtapan del
Oro are preserved details of traditional flavor and its whitewashed
houses have windows and balconies
decorated with multicolored flowers.
One of the best moments to enjoy the
beautiful corners and the kindness of
the people of this town is during one
of its boisterous popular festivities
which are held on September 29th in
honor of the Archangel St. Michael,
the 23rd of February commemorating
the birth of the town, apart from the
Spring Carnival and the commemoration of Easter; during these dates
we can enjoy some of the tasty culi-
nary specialties of this town, such as

*The region where the town is located
has natural spots of great beauty.*

*This street has the façades of houses
painted in white and garnet colors.*

*Simple portal with a small roof
protecting it.*

pozole or mole guajolote, together with drinks such as fermented
blackberry bush or pulque, and to finish, a delicious guava sweet.
Probably, many of the women offering these products will be dressed
with the typical mazahua costume, consisting of a band of brilliant
colors and a knitted blouse. Other samples of their traditions are the
craftsmanship, specially embroidery and linen dresses, the rugs
manufactured in a town workshop, and also furniture and wooden
objects.

At a distance of approximately two kilometers from the center of
town is the ecological park of El Salto, so called for the impressive
cascade of that name that can be admired there. These surroun-

dings have great beauty with semitropical vegetation
and several species of trees, such as ocotes, oaks and
cacahuetes. Along the roads beautiful panoramic
sights surprise us, where nature displays its entire
splendor. This park, equipped with installations
such as the surface barbecues for visitors, covers the
surface of the towns of Ixtapan del Oro and Donato
Guerra, at an altitude of 1800 meters, with an area of
7 hectares and was created in 1987. One of its best
attractions is the famous cascade known as Salto de

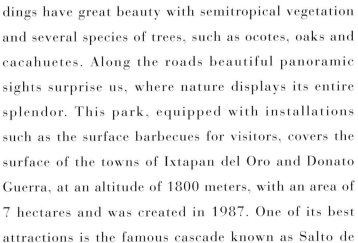

*Life is present in this arcade made
with pilasters and wooden beams.*

Chihuahua, with a drop of 60 meters and its crystal clear water flows into the Ixtapan River that crosses the town; this refreshing scene can be enjoyed from the tables and seats strategically located in front of the cascade.

Other places in the surrounding area worthy of a visit are the El Salitre spa famous for the excellent properties of its waters that have a temperature of 20°C and are distributed amongst several swimming pools. This place is perfectly prepared with cabins for guests and a magnificent garden planted with fruit trees that add to the natural beauty of the surroundings. Also, in this place is located the Zacango zoo and the important archaeological remains of the town of San Miguel Itxapan, where a painting attributed to the Toltecas was found.

If one walks at sunset through the cobbled streets of Ixtapan del Oro, will find a perfect place for meditation and reflection, and if lucky, maybe he or she will see one of the fantastic and beneficial beings capable of incredible feats and who exist in the legends known by the old folks of this incomparable town.

El Oro

T he cold air of the sierra is felt on the skin and the ghost of the precious golden metal walks the streets of what once was the richest mining town in the world, El Oro, and, who knows if still in its depths it hides deposits which escaped the eye of the early miners. The landscape here is conditioned by its location in a mountainous range, 2.748 m over sea level ant its surroundings represent one of the most attractive areas in the State of Mexico, where the town of El Oro is located, because here you can find together deserted lands, warm valleys in the South and mountainous formations where snow makes its presence known. These geographic characteristics of the town make it a privileged spot for the practice of sports, such as motocross and mountain bike riding.

The old mining town, previously named Real de Minas, was founded in the last quarter of the XVIII century in lands property of the

Parroquia del Oro, whose atrium is used by the local residents as place for meetings and celebrations.

One of the most typical streets with balconies which open towards it and decorated with Mexican flags.

Cobbled street with polychromed building façades.

On the following page, *some entrances to businesses in this mining town.*

Tultenango Estate, thanks to an initiative of the first discoverers of the huge treasures hidden inside it. The abundance of gold deposits made it to be considered the richest of the world, comparable to those of Transvaal, in the African Continent. This circumstance served as an inducement for a great number of people who reached the town moved by the desire of wealth and soon the town grew and gained an ever-increasing importance. Its period of splendor came at the end of the XIX century and beginning of the XX century, when deposits of other precious minerals were found given it growing importance until a decree of 1902 raised the town to the rank of city under the name of El Oro de Hidalgo. But, from that moment on, mining of minerals started declining, population began to emigrate and its streets were gradually becoming deserted.

Nowadays it is a pleasure walking through the town, and remembering, gazing among the stones of the sumptuous constructions, the fortunes of other days and the bustling activity that covered with noises its walls. One of the buildings that retains the genuine flavor and characteristics of the age when it was constructed, the most splendorous one for the town, is the Municipal Palace rose at the beginning of the XX century under strong European aesthetic influence, the neoclassic current and the art nouveau. In 1979 a mural painting with the title *El Génesis Minero* was painted for placement in its portico, and in the upper floor halls it is still possible to find the original floors, furniture and velvet drapes in fashion in those days. Another building with similar characteristics and in agreement with the taste of the period is the Teatro Juárez, built between 1906 and 1907, in French neoclassic style in the exterior and art nouveau ornamentation inside, highlighting beautiful

The importance of this town in the mining industry can be confirmed by the presence of installations connected with this activity.

Wooden construction with a stone base.

Interior of church, decorated with gold applications on walls and coverings.

Façade of Teatro Juárez, in which constructions European styles were followed.

El Oro Municipal Palace, with clear reminiscence of European styles.

entrance halls with doors and balconies of carved wood.

There are also earlier constructions, such as the chapels of La Magdalena, Santa María de Guadalupe, Tapaxco and Santiago Oxtempan, the latter built around the XVII century, mining was the reason for other work of great importance for the town, the railroad station and the railway that belonged to the Mexico-Acámbaro line, in order to facilitate transportation of the mined mineral. El Oro was also the place chosen to construct the "Museo de Minería del Estado de México", where you can see tools and machinery used for mining in the XIX century, graphic documents of the process and samples of minerals that were obtained in the abundant mines of the area. Outside the Museum you can still see objects related to the mining activity such as mills, and other installations of the mining companies, near the mines that gave fame to the town, named La Esperanza, La Victoria, La Aurora or El Consuelo, perhaps called that way because of the large quantity of silver, gold, pyrite, manganese and iron which they offered.

The most important festivity of the town was that of carnival, which included a large display of activities such as horse races, car parades, cock fights or charreadas; some of these activities take place on December 12th, the Virgen de Guadalupe Day, when,

Details of building with a great balcony surrounded by plants.

Another view of the municipality with surrounding mountains in the background.

Two storied building with a wide arched gallery on its lower floor.

Peculiar iron structure that reminds us of the miners who worked in El Oro.

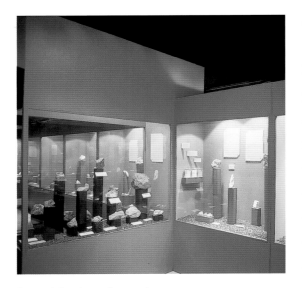

Some of the pieces that can be seen in the Museo de la Minería in this town.

apart from events of religious nature such as processions or pilgrimages, take place. In the street markets which are set up on Mondays at El Oro, it is possible to find among other things handcrafted objects such as textiles, silversmith items, wooden furniture, ceramic or works of popotillo and also typical dishes from all the State of Mexico, like tamales de tuza, el obispo or fruta del horno. Among the interesting places near the town we must mention the Brockman Dam, where you can fish or ride, or the village of Temascalcingo.

Peculiar corner surrounded by flowers and forest.

View of a building which reminds you of European constructions.

Another one of the objects related to mining which are present in this town.

Real de Arriba

MEXICO

In scenery of mountains covered with leafy forests, home of numerous fantastic protagonists of tales and legends, located on the Sierra de
Temascaltepec, which means "Cerro de Baños" (Baths Hill) in náhuatl,
there is a secluded town with a mining tradition where time seems to
have come to a stop. This region is part of what in the XVI century
was the province of La Plata, known for the existence of numerous
mining enclaves. Topography takes different rocky shapes, gorges and
deep ravines, which earnestly protect any silver or gold which may
still remain.

This town, during the prehispanic period was part of a territory
known as Cacalostoc, which means "cueva de cuervos" (Crow's Cave)
and it became a settlement for matlatzincas and later the aztecs. All
of them extracted precious minerals from the mountain veins and the
Vado River, where the fragments of metals were washed to separate

Details of a painted façade, with wooden shutters.

Cheerful polychromed kiosk, in the town square.

151

Many of the homes in Real de Arriba have small wooden roofs in their façades.

them from the earth. This river carries plenty of water and crosses the town. It is formed by the water coming from the melting of snows on the volcano Nevado de Toluca and is later joined by other currents. The fertile lands of Real de Arriba are irrigated by different streams that originate therein, giving the people and the visitors who want to go there, a great variety of trees, flowers and agricultural products.

In the second half of the XVI century Real de Arriba started to be known with the arrival of many people looking for its precious metals; soon it became one of the most important mining centers, contributing to develop other communities to accommodate the great number of people and infrastructures where built in it needed for the mining and treatments of minerals such as stables or mills, of which more than 300 were built. During the XVII and XVIII centuries the mineral continued to make the town a prosperous one, houses were built which evidenced the wealth of their owners, public buildings and a church. However the

Stone wall with access grille and a cross above.

On the following page, the streets of Real de Arriba have a special charm due to the great number of expressive colors, small roofs and cobbled pavements.

Main square with the kiosk and lush vegetation surrounding the town.

XIX century did not bring good times for the town, which saw its mines progressively abandoned because the precious metals were not so easily found; in order to remedy this the government started giving a number of concessions for the exploitation of mines to several North American and British companies. This last action brought a certain relief for the town and its mines, many of which began to produce gold and silver, as El Socorro, La Guitarra, Magdalena, Gachupinas, Santa Ana, Mina Vieja or El Rincón. This exploration companies, particularly the British ones, brought new machinery and techniques that greatly favored the mining operations since 1900. But also this second golden age of the mines ended by 1940, when production decreased completely and the mines have to be closed, provoking the departure of the people who lived from them. Those staying did not give up and began to work in the fields, helped by the abundance of water and the quality of the lands. Soon this town began to be boisterous again, its houses filling up and a new prosperous sector based in agriculture and commerce of their products with the nearby region was developed.

Real de Arriba has all the charm of the old mining towns and still retains signs of the economic prosperity which it enjoyed, the walls of the houses are painted in lively and attractive colors and are particularly noticeable some houses built in the XIX century as a symbol of wealth. A plaque with the inscription located in the Hoz Bridge, at the entrance of the town, reminds you of the start of the mining exploitation in Real de Arriba in the middle of the XVI century. Its main square is like in many other towns, a meeting place for residents, and a kiosk is built therein, and next to it is the church built in the

The tones of their façades stand out among the greenness of the mountains where this town is located.

The streets painted in lively colors witnessed a heavy mining activity which took over this town in a past period.

Another happy corner of Real de Arriba.

Details of the remarkable Baroque façade of the church, built in the XVIII century.

XVII century and which harmonizes baroque elements that reach the maximum expression of churrigueresco. Its façade is baroque, with two bodies, an access with a half point arch and niches carved for housing sculptures. From the outside it is worth admiring the great tower that shelters the bells and ends in a cross shape; the interior has a nave and is remarkable a baroque altarpiece of golden wood, with the Virgen de los Dolores and a crucifix. Other religious buildings from the XVIII century are the cemetery chapel and the church of San Mateo Almoloya, with elements that reinterpret past aesthetic currents such as the renaissance. Many of the objects used in previous centuries in the mining of minerals can still be seen in this town, maybe waiting patiently for someone who will give them their former use: tools, machinery and even a mill. The remains of estates and mines are also preserved; there is one known as El Rincón, one of the most important ones in the first part of the XX century, has fragments of walls that were part of the installations and dwellings of the miners, and another estate called El Polvorín, also called La Providencia.

Ayapango

W hen we visit Ayapango for the first time we receive the impression of having been there before, of recognizing its walls and the light reflected on them. This must be due to the fact that some of the buildings and corners of the town, such as the Santa María ranch or the Hacienda de Retana has been chosen as locations for many Mexican films because of their beauty and typical characteristics. This simple place of houses decorated with original designs that have survived, full of history and linked to the lives of many well celebrities, is located on the western slope of the Iztaccihuatl.

Its name is derived from the word *eyapango*, formed by *ey*, which means three, and by *apantli*, translated as channel or stream; maybe this name was due to the old presence of systems of conducts used for irrigation purposes. Early in the XX century was born here Gabriel Ramos Millán, who held various political positions, promoted the arts

Simple altar presided by a golden altarpiece and religious images.

Building of the Municipal Presidency, that can be entered by a stair case.

159

protecting several artists and around the middle of the century received from the President the task of creating the National Corn Commission, which favored the distribution of space and promoted investigations to improve the quality of seeds. In memory of this important person the town added his name to its, calling itself Ayapango de Gabriel Ramos Millán. The affection felt by the population also materialized itself in the names given to the primary school and to an important street, apart from ordering a bust that was placed near the kiosk, and the portrait destined to the Municipal Palace. Also in this town was born, centuries before, in 1430, the poet *Aquiauhtzin Cuauhquiyahuacatzintli*, and a name that was adopted by the Casa de la Cultura. It is very common that many buildings and lots of Ayapango have come to be known by original nahua denominations used by prehispanic inhabitants of these lands; thus we will

Old railroad tracks crossing the town.

find reference to places such as *Tepetlipa, Caliecac, Huitzila* o *Xaltepa*, which manage to keep in the memory of History the town and its people's past. The street are exquisitively cobbled and the houses retain the local tradition of split roofs with flat tiles of dark clay that are attractive and remind us of other European locations. Many of the houses were built at the end of the XIX century and beginning of the XX, so that many decorating elements and details reflect the tastes of the period. Buildings such as La Casa Afrancesada and La Casa Grande, which has interesting architectural features, are worthy of a leisured visit.

Porch with the characteristic black tiles used in the houses of Ayapango.

The main church in town is that of Santiago Apóstol, belonging to the former convent of that name, the atrium of the construction has trees and is surrounded with typical details used in many constructions of the colonial period. The front of the church is delicately decorated, reflecting the hands of local artists. Other interesting churches located in local branches of Ayapango are San Bartolo

On the following page, the main façade of the church in the former convent of Santiago Apóstol.

Façade of the Casa de Cultura, a building that has elements of Gothic and Islamic styles.

Details of the façade of the former convent of Santiago Apóstol, with characteristic elements of local influence.

Some of the streets in this town receive names of historic personalities of Mexico, as evidenced by the billboards in this picture.

Mihuacán, San Dieguito Chalcatepehuacan, San Cristóbal Poxtla or San Juan Tlamapa. The convent of El Calvario was inhabited by the Fransciscan Order and built on grounds of volcanic characteristics; its decay has caused the destruction of many of its sections, but, those remaining give us an idea of the original appearance of this building. Other building, very damaged by age and of which only ruins remain, but that has contributed to the chronicle of the town, is the former Estate of Santa Cruz Tamariz.

House surrounded by wall with a tiled porch.

Apart from the agricultural activity, this town is famous for the preparation of delicious cheeses and dairy products of great quality, which are exported to several parts of the country; those best known are the one manufactured in the farm of El Lucero, which also can be a attractive place to visit, apart from giving you the opportunity to taste whatever is produced there.

Tepotzlán

I t is one of the most impacting towns in Mexico, its hugeness leaves one without words, in its universe are mingled history, nature, art and culture as if they were the four sacred elements, water, earth, air and fire, and they bewitch us forever claiming a niche in our memory. Ever thing there is sacred, the valley was the birthplace of prince *Tepoztécatl*, son of the god of air *Ehécatl* and *Chimalma* and is surrounded by mountainous formations among which we can find the hill that takes its name from the son of the wind and where, according to the legend, he still lives watching the valley from his rocky altar dedicated to the gods *Quetzalcóatl* and *Huitzilopochtli* who are represented by the sun and the moon.

The name of the town originates from Indian words that have several meaning as "lugar del cobre" (place of copper), "lugar de hachas" (place of axes) or "lugar de piedras quebradas" (place of broken stones); the mountain formations that surround it still retain the carved

Façade of the Tepotzlán convent, with its front flanked by two towers.

The beauty of the views around this town impress those who witness them.

167

Fragment of façade painted in red and with small wooden roof.

figures with enigmatic meanings that were created by the prehispanic dwellers and that have to do with the religion and beliefs of these people. This territory was occupied from the Preclassic to the Postclassic period and one of the races who lived there was the Tlahuica in the chronological period spanning between the abandonment of Teotihuacán and the foundation of Tenochtitlán. The *Mendoza Codex* tells that during the middle of the XV century the aztecs conquered the region where Tepoztlán was located and at the end of that century the mysterious temple established on the highest part of the Tepoztécatl or Tepozteco hill was constructed, with Aztec construction characteristics and became a landmark for devotion and pilgrimage for the prehispanic cultures.

The incredible beauty and peace of the scenery surrounding the town seems to seep through into its streets, whitewashed houses and buildings,

In this façade it is possible to see other decorating objects made by residents of the town.

One of the many craftsmen who create authentic works of art with their hands.

An original corner combining faith and the beauty of its surroundings.

One of the most important
prehispanic remains of the area is
the temple decorating with low
reliefs of enigmatic meaning.

Another view of the archeological
remains found in Tepozteco Hill.

Popular tradition and the
inspiration of its craftsmen get
together in this lively spot.

Details of the open gallery at the Tepóztlan convent.

Town street, with one of the surrounding mountains in the background.

such as the Palace of Justice and the Presidential, its fountains, parks and its main square with the superb convent of the Nativity of the Virgin and its church, built between 1560 and 1580 coming towards it. Some years before brother Domingo de la Anunciación came to this place and created a settlement for Dominican monks, who gave impulse to this great architectural work that is now part of the route of the Convents of the State of Morelos. The establishment has one of the oldest cloisters in Mexico, and its construction presents peculiarities that provide with originality such as the presence of the porter's office integrated in the same body where the chapel rests on the left side. There are still remains of what once was an open chapel and of mural paintings on the walls of the convent. In the lower cloister there is a pretty washbasin and the upper floor offers a marvelous view of the surrounding landscape from its viewpoint the nave of the church is covered by a huge cannon dome, the presbytery with crossed domes and its front is notable for the skill of the decorating plateresque details, such as little angels, stars or shields. In the tympanum there are images of the Virgin with the Child between Saints Catalina and Domingo.

On Wednesdays and Sundays, a folkloric open market called tiangui is established in the main square, which relates to the culture of the prehispanic peoples and that was used to trade products of different places. In this lively market you can find attractive things, local crafts and products for daily use. Behind the convent, during the XVI century, were erected several constructions to store grain which were later used by Carlos Pellicer to install his Archeological Museum; this person loved the land of Tepoztlán deeply, dedicated poems to it and contributed

On the following page, a wall painting serves as a billboard for several businesses.

Access staircase to the porch of this home.

172

Through the half opened door you can see the beautiful green colors in the surrounding area.

to the obtaining of drinking water and the construction of a church; the Museum was formed with items and graphic documents which he donated. The sections that can be visited cover samples of Olmeca or Mayan culture, items from pilgrims who visited the temple and some found in the archeological zone of the town.

The climb towards the summit of the Tepozteco starts at the Cruz del Bautisterio, the place where according to legend was baptized the lord of Tepoztlán in 1538 after his conversion to Christianity. Further up there are three figures carved on the rock and called Las Tres Marías and before you reach the summit, another colossal form, 30 m in height, called El Muñeco or Los Gemelos, because of its shape. Next to it, we find a narrow alley leading to the entrance of the archeological zone at the summit, where there is a temple dedicated to *Tepoztécatl*, a sacred being associated with the farming of maguey and the preparation for pulque. It has two rooms decorated with enigmatic relieves that represent the Four Directions of the Universe or the Four Cosmological Suns.

The character of its people and the silent pride of belonging to a race governed by a king who is descendant of the gods can be seen on their

Details of the wonderful frescoes that took shape in the local convent.

On the following page, the brilliant polychrome of façades, doors and windows, important element of this community.

Corner in Tepoztlán, with grill work in most of the bays.

174

Some of the most important
handicrafts in this town are the
ceramic and clay objects.

Another façade, full of color and folklore.

The vivid colors of the façades reach
the kiosk at the square. It has
beautiful grillwork.

Mexican flags fill this corner across

the municipal palace.

Façade of the church, flanked by

towers of different heights.

faces, it is manifested during the most important festivity of Tepoztlán, its Patron Saint Day, celebrated on September 7 and 8, when the Birth of Mary is commemorated as well as the memory of their king who was converted to Christianity. On these dates a portal made of several seeds is prepared with different themes every year and placed in the atrium of the church. On the night of September 7, the festivities start with a pilgrimage to the summit of the Tepozteco, joined by torches, which light up the way, thus creating an unreal, fantastic image. When you reach the top, the human warmth, the feeling of sharing a common origin and the happy mood contribute to make the food and appetizers that are served, taste delicious. The next days, there are continuous shows of affection towards the Virgin, typical songs (las mañanitas), offering, and dances that last all day, until night when the conflict between El Señor de Tepostán and the neigh-

Curious decoration of a façade in

Tepoztlán.

Cobbled street of the municipality.

boring towns, due to his conversion to Christianity, is scenified.

Other well-known and colorful celebrations take place during carnival, when local residents and visitors forget their sorrows happily dancing the famous Brinco del Chinelo. If there is a town in Mexico which claim heritage of the sacred and transcendental and which changes our mood with only a slight effort, it is sure to be Tepoztlán.

Cuautla

C uautla or *Kuahtlan*, whose etymology comes from *Kuah-uitl*, which means "tree" and of *tlan-tli*, translated as "plentiful" and that has two meanings, "wood or forest" and "close to the eagles", is a place rewarded by nature with beautiful landscapes and a great number of beneficial water springs which give it the name of the City of Spas. These springs and the muddy ground in this zone were the reasons why it was uninhabited when the first Spaniards arrived and why the nearest community was settled in nearby Xochimilkatziko, where the oldest archaeological remains of this territory have been found.

This place appears linked to Oaxtepec in the *Matrícula de Tributos* and in the *Códice Mendocino*, having become part of the Marquisate of Oaxaca Valley during the colonial period and having been evangelized starting with the foundation of the Convent of Santo Domingo around the middle of the XVI century. The widespread sugar cane

Simple corner of one of the churches of this town, presided by Christ on the cross.

Cuautla street, with lined shops showing their signs and billboards.

181

fields gave the area great prosperity and this along with the important constructions of the religious orders favored the awarding of the rank of jurisdiction to Cuautla, heading one of the two largest mayorships of the State of Morelos in 1810. Also in this place took place one of the most important events of the Mexican Independence, the so called Siege of Cuautla, during which, General Calleja, in his campaign against the insurgents attacks Morelos on February 19th, 1812 and after been defeated decides to besiege Cuautla, its inhabitants resisted during 72 days until the second of May when Morelos breaks through the surge, obtaining a victory and opening new roads towards independence. In commemoration of the siege of Cuautla a decree of 1829 established that from that moment the city should be called The Heroic City of Morelos in 1881, the railroad reaches Cuautla, which became an important communication route and during the revolutionary period, it would again be sieged by Emiliano Zapata, whose body was buried in the municipal pantheon and in 1935 his remains transferred to an urn next to the statue placed in the square of the Revolución del Sur.

All these historical episodes have left their mark on the streets, squares and buildings of the town, such as the main church, dedicated to the apostle James, which is the church and former convent of Santo Domingo de

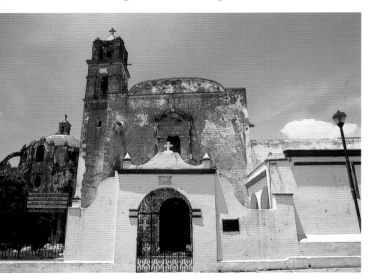

Guzmán, known by this name because the friars of this order lived there during the XVI century. Another former convent and its church is that of San Diego, located in the spot where the Dominican monks built a chapel in the XVI century, and later, in the middle of the XVII century the discalced Franciscan monks called "dieguinos" raised a convent with two cloisters which represents one of the most important architectural works in Cuautla. In the high cloister is located the museum José María Morelos y Pavón, dedicated to the siege of Cuautla and with four halls where are exhibited uniforms, coins, models, photographs and documents about the events of this period. Another interesting church is that of the Señor del Pueblo, so called because it

Details of a store in this town, where
you can purchase books and
magazines.

The intensive historic and social
activity of this town is reflected in
this expressive mural painting.

Bustling corner where the stores
display their merchandise outdoors.

contains in its interior an image of Christ in the Cross, known by that name. In it, performances are carried out on the second Friday of Lent, and as the other former convents it was occupied during the siege of Cuautla.

During the fire that took place in 1911 the Municipal Palace suffered great damages, this being the place where Zapatas's remains were kept before their transfer to the square; the bell known as Nuestra Señora de Dolores was the only thing left of the Gualupita Chapel after the events of the siege and today is kept in this place. Also in Cuautla we can visit the old railroad station, built in land belonging to the convent of San Diego and inaugurated in June 1881; the line was originally called Ferrocarril de Morelos and later incorporated to the Ferrocarril Interoceánico de México-Veracruz. Today still operates a narrow track steam engine no. 279, the only one in the country, built by Baldwing Locomotive Works of Philadelphia for Ferrocarriles Nacionales de México, which was put in service in 1904. Across the main

On the following page, *details of an irregular brick adornment.*

square of this town there is another museum that delights the visitor, the Histórico del Oriente de Morelos, also known as Casa de Morelos, having been occupied by this General during the siege; the building was declared national monument in 1832, in 1949 became a regional museum having suffered several changes to the present times, when it is knows as Museo Histórico. It has 13 halls where several objects are displayed from the prehispanic era to the evangelization or independence.

The existence of waters with beneficial properties has permitted the presence of numerous spas in this area; one of the best known is that of Agua Hedionda, that due to the great concentration of sulphates in its water is known worldwide. Also in this area there are many nurseries where plants and fruit trees are grown and requested from numerous parts of the country. Life in the streets decorated with many flowers seems to increase their color when women walk by, wearing their typical dress, the *tetelcinga*, consisting of a *huipil* and a dark blue skirt tightened by a red or blue band; this dress is said to be an Olmeca heritage as well as the tradition of painting the hair red, green or blue. These traditional dresses can be seen mainly during the celebration of the numerous popular festivities of the region, such as the fair on the second Friday of lent, in honor of the siege of Cuautla between the 19th of February and the 2nd of May, the 29th and the 30th of September when the principal festivity in commemoration of General Morelos's birth is held or the cultural events of Jornadas Altamiranas which take place in November. In these festivities are also shown objects of craftsmanship made by the inhabitants among which are important the birdcages, the *huaraches* and the sandals.

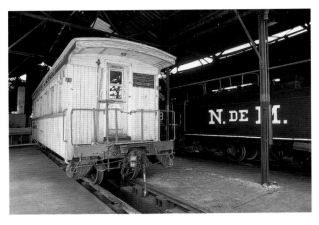

View of the old railroad station.

Some of the trains still to be seen at the Cuautla railroad station are true historic relics.

Beautiful façade of the Municipal Palace decorated with the colors of the Mexican flag.

Papantla

The history and background of this legendary populations are known through ther traditions and prehispanic remains that exist in the surrounding area.

T here is a story that tells that, from a place and at a date which are not important, arrived at Papantla a foreign traveler who remained there some time, during which he used to wander indefatigably along the streets breathing deeply; many years later this same traveler, back in his home town and very near death told a relative that with age all his memory had been erased except the indescribable smell of vanilla which he had enjoyed during his visit to Papantla and that had remained with him all his life as one of his most pleasant memories which he connected with his childhood, when he used to eat desserts and ice creams with this ingredient. The fact is that this place is the main producer of vanilla in the country, and with the passing of time, the stones, the walls, the streets and even the people, carry the smell that fills up the soul.

View of the bustling veracruzan town.

On the following page, *stores,
houses and decorating elements such
as the fountain at the entrance
of town.*

Before the colonial period it belonged, together
with the surrounding territory, to the Mexicas
and its name derived from Nahua is translated
as "lugar de papán" which is a bird that lives in
the area, although the Totonacas called it "luna
buena" (good moon). Until 1935 it was known
as Papantla de Hidalgo, at which time it chan-
ged its name to Papantla de Olarte, in memory
of Serafín Olarte. Its coat of arms has a roun-
ded four-sided shape in its bottom part, similar
to the Totonaca yokes; it is divided in four parts
that represent the four boroughs of Papantla,
San Juan, Santa Cruz, Zapote and Naranjo. On
its surface appear symbols and images which are
characteristics of the town, such as the Danza de
los Voladores, the vanilla plant, the pyramid of
El Tajín, important sacred city located near
Papantla, references to Totonaco nobility and

*Details of the upper floor of a
building formed by a gallery with
arches.*

sculptures, such as the three sacred hearts originating from tu tu and nacu which mean three and
heart, as well as signs of Náhuatl origin relative to
its past.

The small houses of Papantla present a homogene-
ous aspect, with its walls of white adobe and its divided roofs formed by red tiles; the main square is an
interesting place where many fascinating festive
celebrations are held. Also the atrium of the church
of Nuestra Señora de la Asunción, flooded with flowers, seeds and fruits during the offering made at
the festivity of the Voladores. Also deserving a visit
is the mural painting by Teodoro Cano that can be
seen in the building of the Presidencia Municipal
and represents the Mexican people.

This town acquires a solemn aspect, which is
impressive, silent, sacred, when its people fill the
streets during the celebration of Corpus Christi, a
festivity whose origins are found in the prehispanic
period and that took place for the first time in 1550.

*Street in Papantla, where old
constructions are mingled with more
modern houses.*

*This house has two stories and the
top one has a long balcony protected
by a small roof*

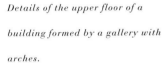

The building in this picture has a top formed by a frieze inspired in classic models.

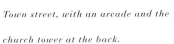

Town street, with an arcade and the church tower at the back.

The celebrations begin with La Mayor, at which time those participating in the Danza del Volador cut the trunk along which they would climb and carry it through the mountains to the atrium of the church, where it would be placed, next to the offering, the streets welcome the procession that come from all neighborhoods, all destined to meet at the church, where a long mass will be held, which is followed with continue its way among canticles and blessings the men who will climb the stick will be dressed in typical dresses, consisting of trousers that are tied above the ankle and a white colored blouse decorated with lace; they are five; representing the four cardinal points and a priest, in a ceremony in honor of the Sun. The fliers (voladores) climb slowly and then jump forward, suspended by the feet, and remain twisting during moments that seem endless due to the sacred nature of the event. These men are chosen by a council of elders at the age of 13 and subsequently, when they stop performing the ritual at age 30 they will teach others how to do it.

This show is the best known, but during the celebrations there are also fireworks, music and dance, such as the one of Los Negritos; in memory of the tears shed by a mother who suffers because her daughter has been bitten by a snake that of the Santiagueros or the Moros y Cristianos. On August 15th is celebrated the Asunción (Assumption)

One of the voladores of Papantla, participating along with others in the famous danza de los voladores.

Magnificent kiosk of great proportions, that can be reached by the stairs.

194

This territory to which Papantla belongs was a subject to the Mëxican Empire and in it numerous remains of the various cultures that inhabited it can be found.

The façade of this house has beautiful friezes with vegetal subjects framing doors and windows.

and besides the typical dances takes place the coronation of a queen of the festivities, based on the old tradition, and the feast of the vanilla called Festival *Xanath*. A particularly colorful and eye-catching celebration takes place on the Día de Difuntos, when there is a competition of altars made of rocks, wood, fruits, flowers and everything that the imagination of the owner can produce. Vanilla, so important as it is for the town folk, is used also to prepare some typical handicraft objects, as the plaited figures that represent animals, flowers or religious images. There are also musical instruments of wood and squirrel skin used to play at gathering and parties.

The significance of the Danza de los Voladores, known and associated with the town of Papantla for centuries is related to the important ritual celebrations that took place among the indigenous dwellers of this region with regard to the calendar and the Sun; the dancers were disguised as birds with feathers of brilliant colors. The trunk, climbed by the Voladores represents the fifth point of earth besides the cardinal ones, and dances take place around it while asking forgiveness from the god of Monte Quihuicolo for having chopped it. Also, help is begged from the god of wind to favor the flight of the dancers, who must take 13 turns of the trunk, these turns, multiplied by four, became 52, which is a magical number representing the coming cycle of the new sun.

Several stores united by a common façade with a small roof of wood and tiles.

Through a half point arch you can see the façade and one of the windows across the street.

Tlacochahuaya

T lacochahuaya is a quiet and friendly town, encased in a beautiful landscape and where its people receive neighbors and foreigners with a wide smile full of light. It was the place chose by the Dominicans to built the extraordinary convent and complex in the XVI century, which is today one of the most important colonial jewels of Mexico. It is located close to the city of Oaxaca (16 km); surrounded by other beautiful towns and in it you can enjoy the popular traditions of the State of Oaxaca.

Its name originates from a word in Náhuatl, which means "wet land" and was founded by a Zapoteco warrior named *Cochicahuala*, which means "he who fights at night". Its streets and buildings still retain the local and colonial elements which gave place to the present configuration of Tlacochahuaya. The construction of the Dominican convent started halfway through the XVI century and

Pavilion that takes advantage of the corner wall, topped by a dome.

Beautiful view of the kiosk in the main square, surrounded by colorful plants and flowers.

The woman in the picture carries a bundle on her head, a traditional way to carry objects.

Window of a façade protected by a grill.

the work lasted until the beginning of the XVII century. It has rather unusual characteristic for religious constructions of this nature, which is due to the fact that it was planned as a place for meditation and seclusion, selecting for this purpose the beauty and quietness of this Oaxaqueña town. For these same reasons, the complex was built with simple and sober structures, although the magnificent artists who worked in it left the mark of their genius in the decoration; the local details introduced by local artists of the area are present in the decoration as well as in the construction elements. It was dedicated to San Jerónimo as representative of a secluded and austere live, one that was practiced by some of the personalities involved in the construction and everyday life of the convent, as brother Jordán de Santa Catalina and brother Juan de Córdoba.

The church has a main floor in the shape of a Latin cross covered by a cannon vault and a dome in the transept zone. The attractive decoration, which fills the interior with baroque and plateresque motifs, includes little angels, vases, flowers or leaves. There are also superb works of art which include the paintings and sculptures which belong to the altarpieces of the church. One of the most

Boisterous meeting of animals in a yard.

Store, in a simple façade; next to it is a cat.

Concrete cloister, of small
dimensions and formed by two
floors.

Cobbled street and wall topped in a
way to resemble a fortress.

Impressive view inside the church of
the Convent of San Jerónimo,
covered with remarkable mural
paintings.

remarkable is the one dedicated to the Virgin of Guadalupe, made in 1689, with the participation of Josep Herrera; in it there are several paintings dedicated to the life of the Virgin. Other important aspects of its interior are the mural paintings made at the end of the XVII century, which feature stars, flowers and suns, the beautiful organ located in the choir manufactured in 1739, with a decoration harmonizing with the agricultural structure of the church, the altarpieces made in the first quarter of the XVII century by Juan de Arrúe and the pulpit. The main façade has two towers that contain the bells and the entrance is in baroque style; it has pilasters, niches for sculptures and a pediment, the most outstanding image being that of San Jerónimo. The symbol of the Dominicans, two small dogs, is carved on the keystone of the arch at the entrance. There is a side entrance, more simple and where you can see the Virgin of Guadalupe.

In spite of the simplicity of its construction, this convent looks impressive as you advance along the great open esplanade that surrounds it and that enhances its attraction. The atrium has two entrances, it is limited by a bard and has an atrium cross; it is worth mentioning the two chapels and a sun clock. In the Southern side of the church there is a cloister, consisting of two stories, and the cells for the monks are specially dark and small.

The Municipal Palace of the town has in its main façade a portico and on the corners there are curious golden lions with very characteristic red jaws. In this town there remains something which is very unusual to see today, the pillory which has been there for centuries and where the condemned men where publicly exhibited. The people of Tlacochahuaya gather in the square to chat about the events of the day to sell theirs agricultural products and handicrafts, which

Colorful flowers decorating the streets of Tlacothahuaya.

Façade painted in colors with bays highlighted with mouldings and pilasters.

Interior of a gallery formed by half point arches over pilasters, in the Convent of San Jerónimo.

Façade with grille which gives access to a suggestive garden.

View of the magnificent group formed by the Convent of San Jerónimo, one of the construction jewels of this town.

have art characteristic for having been manufactured with several raw materials. The square, together with the rest of the houses, dresses up for the popular festivities, such as those in honor of the patron San Jerónimo or the ones that take place in July, known as Lunes del Cerro; in all of them there are horse races, fireworks and dances, although the most remarkable thing is the joy and humor of its people, who share antojitos along with the beer, pulque, tepache or mescal. The main dishes that can be tasted here are tamales of black mole or the meats with chile sauce. Among others, one of the most characteristic and curious elements is the mole that is prepared with over 30 ingredients and is different depending of the products used. Also famous in the whole State are the chapulines colorados, small grasshoppers which are main character of a legend that states that those who try them will go back to Oaxaca. To conclude an excellent meal, you must try the tasty desserts and, among them those prepared with delicious fruits.

Details of a brick construction which was blocked off.

206